Daily Guided Writing

Carol Simpson

Illustrated by Amy O'Brien Krupp

Good Year Books
Parsippany, New Jersey

Acknowledgments

I wish to thank the following students whose pieces of writing appear within the pages of this book. Their enthusiasm for writing keeps me excited about teaching the often difficult process. Thank you, too, to their parents for giving me permission to use their work.

Kirsten Bruns   Megan Johnson   Kyle Polite   Amanda Wright
Emilee Goad   Nikki Merz   Megan Ollman

Dedication

Thank you to Sandy McCombs, a second-grade teacher whose students helped me to practice some of what I preach in this book. Thank you to Mary Stevens and Dee Westergren, my fellow Title 1 teachers at Steele Accelerated School, who were willing to try the language-rich, first-grade pull-out program that I suggested we try. I think they see the value of writing the morning news with at-risk emergent readers.

Good Year Books

are available for most basic curriculum subjects plus many enrichment areas. For more Good Year Books, contact your local bookseller or educational dealer. For a complete catalog with information about other Good Year Books, please write:

Good Year Books
An imprint of Pearson Learning
299 Jefferson Road
Parsippany, New Jersey 07054-0480
1-800-321-3106
www.pearsonlearning.com

Design by AOK Design.
Text copyright © 1998 Carol Simpson.
Illustrations copyright © 1998 Good Year Books, an imprint of Addison-Wesley
    Educational Publishers, Inc.
All Rights Reserved.
Printed in the United States of America

ISBN 0-673-36402-X

4 5 6 7 8 9 - MH - 06 05 04 03 02 01 00

Preface

The purpose of this book is to assist those elementary teachers who feel they need some additional ideas for teaching their students how to become good writers. The ability to communicate with pencil and paper, or word processor, is an important skill for our fast-paced world. As teachers, we realize that not everyone who comes into our classrooms will grow up to become famous authors or journalists. We do know, however, that our students need to be able to communicate in writing in order to be successful adults. This book will hopefully give teachers some additional ideas on how to incorporate several types of guided writing lessons into their daily schedules.

I want to credit my own experiences after more than 25 years in primary classrooms, kindergarten through grade four, with helping me to discover what works! I am encouraged by the writings of experts in the field of education such as Lucy Calkins, Donald Graves, Don Holdaway, and Regie Routman. They write in support of the reading/writing connection, which makes those of us who "try something new" feel more at ease and confident when explaining the "how-tos" and the "whys" to our superiors. Regie Routman writes from her own personal classroom experiences in a way that we can easily understand. We can learn from her successes and follow her lead in helping our children develop into literate, lifelong learners.

The ability to be flexible, and sometimes brave, has led to many wonderful experiences with young children taking risks and demonstrating what creative young people they can be. Imaginations run free when children know they can write down whatever they want to tell others. Guided writing lessons have proven to be an important part of the school day, enabling children to become fluent with pencil and paper.

As a teacher both in primary classrooms and in a Title 1 capacity, I am very proud of the children with whom I work. The results that they have demonstrated in their writing, after having been instructed in guided writing in some form every day, encourage me to continue. Whether I guide them in writing the morning news or an experience story, or critique their journal entries, it is well worth the time I spend on the lessons. I hope that you will try some of my suggestions. I encourage you to share your positive experiences with your colleagues. Spread the word about the value of daily guided writing.

Along with the three chapters on guided writing lessons, you will find an Appendix at the end of this book. The Appendix contains helpful hints for publishing students' stories as well as reproducible news pages and story starters meant to help your young writers.

Contents

From *Daily Guided Writing.* Text © Carol Simpson and Illustrations © Good Year Books.

Introduction

What Is a Guided Writing Lesson?

A guided writing lesson is one in which the teacher demonstrates for students the process of writing a sentence or paragraph using proper English conventions. Students are then given opportunities to show that they can use these strategies and conventions in their own work. Guided writing lessons can be taught as early as kindergarten and should continue for as long as new styles of writing are being expected of students. The guided writing lesson in kindergarten is obviously going to be very different from that taught to a 14-year-old who will write his or her first term paper.

Guided writing lessons include instruction in spelling, sentence structure, use of punctuation and capitalization, quotation marks, and other English conventions. We can also instruct our students in selecting content to include in their paragraphs and stories. We can demonstrate writing a story beginning, middle, and end. Along with sequencing, we can guide the writing of detailed information and descriptive language to make our stories and paragraphs more colorful and interesting.

Guiding and explaining writing strategies and conventions takes time to do, but the benefits will be seen in other written work. The carryover into other writing activities will become evident in the days and months ahead. Demonstrating correct writing procedures will show students what we might expect them to do when they write on their own. If guided writing instruction begins at an early age and follows consistently year after year, perhaps our students will feel more confident when we ask them to write those special reports in their later years of schooling.

1

What Kinds of Writing Can I Guide?

Experience Stories

The primary classroom (kindergarten through second grade) is a place of discovery. The teachers in these classrooms need to make use of opportunities to write about the new ideas and experiences that come up every day. We have all asked students for their thoughts on these shared ideas and experiences that they then wrote down for everyone to read. We used our big chart paper and took simple dictation from the children as they gave us the facts, the details, and the events that they remembered from the new idea or experience. We know that these experience stories can be used for a lot more than simple dictation, reading, and rereading. Instead of just taking the dictation, we can demonstrate how to write down what we say, explain the use of punctuation and capitalization, and ask questions about the text in order to make complete sentences. An explanation of using experience stories for guided writing follows in Chapter 1.

The Daily News

Many primary teachers write a message to their students each day. It may include a simple explanation of what will be taking place that day in the classroom. Sometimes information is included about special school programs or subject matter, which might include local, national, or world news. If the teacher always has the daily news written on the chalkboard prior to the students walking in the door, perhaps he or she should try using the news as a guided writing lesson instead. There are many benefits to taking the time to write the news in front of, and with, the students each day. An in-depth discussion of writing the daily news is included in Chapter 2.

Journal Writing

Many primary teachers incorporate daily journal writing in their classrooms. At a specified time each day, students throughout the primary grades take out their notebooks or journal folders and write for a period of time. Some will write "stories" and others will write whatever pops into their heads. They may write about something that happened at home the night before. They may write about their pet, their baby brother or sister, or their parents and grandparents. They may create a new fictitious character, perhaps an invisible friend. The subject matter is limitless. There is a great opportunity to look at the writing in the journals, pull examples from what we see within the pages, and then guide a lesson in how to improve or change what is written. If journal writing is done every day, allow time immediately afterward for sharing what is written. Use this sharing time once a week to pull anonymous journal examples to edit and critique with the children. Chapter 3 offers suggestions on using journals for guided writing lessons.

Experience Stories

Experience stories are written by a group of students who have shared in the same adventure or experience. Teachers are discovering that the experience stories their children dictate to them can be read, reread, and used to teach conventions of the English language. The guided writing lessons in primary classrooms will vary in skill level and length of text. A kindergarten experience story might contain only sentences that begin with the words "(Student's name) said. . . ." Because of time constraints, each child will probably not have a sentence to dictate for each experience story. The teacher will need to make sure to include all children over a period of time and within a variety of experience stories.

A positive feature of experience stories is that the subject matter is limitless. A group or classroom of students can certainly write an experience story about a field trip they shared. And they can also write a group or class story when they have experienced something un- usual together. For example, students can write about the experience of watching a bird build a nest outside the classroom window. They can write an experience story about the pet hedge- hog that visited their classroom. The teacher who allows for incidental learning—learning that "just happens" without advance planning—will be able to find a topic for an experience story writing lesson at least once a week. Class experience stories can be about very simple events, such as everyone hearing the same loud sound and then wondering what it could be!

Sample Kindergarten Lessons

The guided writing lesson using an experience story in a kindergarten classroom should take place when the children have just shared a memorable experience, such as a field trip to a fire station. After the shared experience, kindergartners dictate their thoughts to the teacher, who writes down what is said. Each child who contributes a sentence to the experience story is asked to come up and write his or her name at the beginning of the sentence they dictated. The teacher might take the opportunity to spell children's names together. A sample lesson might sound like this:

Teacher: We have just had a good time visiting the fire department. Who can tell me something they want to remember about our trip?

Ben: The fire trucks have loud sirens.

Teacher: That's right! Help me write that down. Ben, can you come up here and write your name on our story paper? (Ben writes his name in the appropriate place on the chart paper.) Boys and girls, let's look at Ben's name and say the letters together. (Everyone spells Ben's name aloud.) Good job, Ben. Let's look at the way Ben has written his name. How many of you put a capital letter at the beginning of your name? (All students should raise their hands.) We should all put a capital letter on our name because names are special words. We don't need to make every letter in our name a capital letter, though. What letter is a capital in Ben's name? (B) Are the other letters written as capitals? (No.) Ben has written his name the way I want you to write your name. You should have only one capital letter, the first letter of your name. Here is what Ben wants us to remember about our field trip. (Teacher says the words as he or she writes them on the chart paper.) Ben, can you read what it says? (Teacher helps Ben read that "Fire trucks have loud sirens.")

From *Daily Guided Writing.* Text © Carol Simpson and illustrations © Good Year Books.

As each child who dictated a sentence writes his or her name (probably no more than three or four children), the other students spell or chant the letters and talk about the first letter being the only capital letter. The teacher asks if any other students have a name that starts like Ben's (or whoever has written a name on the chart paper). When the experience story is completed, the teacher guides the students in reading the story aloud. Together they look carefully at the words to find any that are repeated. The word *fire* might appear several times in a story about the fire station. The teacher points to it and asks if anyone sees it written anywhere else in the story. The word is circled each time it appears.

Students can look for other words that begin with or contain the letter *f* and underline those words. The teacher should look for high-frequency words that some students already know how to read.

Teacher: Does anyone see a word they know how to read?

Student: I see the word *big*.

Teacher: How do you know that the word is *big*?

Student: I know that *big* starts with *b* like Ben's name.

Teacher: That's right! Say the word *big* slowly. What sound do you say at the end? (Hopefully, someone says /g/.) What letter stands for the /g/ sound? (G)

The teacher can then talk at an appropriate level about letters and sounds. Those children who are ready for letter/sound associations will perhaps try their hand at writing letters that they think they hear when they want to label a related picture they have drawn. Those who are not yet ready to discover that letters stand for sounds will hopefully benefit from the exposure to the concept at a later time when another experience story is written with the class. *The important thing is to be consistent* with guided writing practices. Use guided writing as often as possible and repeat the skill lessons on a regular basis.

Besides the sample experience story described above, kindergartners can help the teacher, as a group, in writing a class "story" that will be illustrated and put into a class book. Imagine that a classroom of kindergartners has just heard the story *Swimmy* by Leo Leoni. The story ends with the little fishes swimming together in the shape of a big fish and scaring the giant tuna away. The children and their teacher brainstorm ideas for a new story about a little fish. The teacher writes down the ideas and then reads them back to the children. If the sentences make sense and are in a reasonable sequence, the teacher writes the sentences on a large sheet of chart paper. When the teacher does this, he or she might put a blank space in the place where some very important and obvious words in the text should be. The children "read" the story together and decide what the missing words might be. They then write the words in the blank spaces, with the teacher's help.

In the following example, the word *fish* might be used in the first two blank spaces. The children can decide what other words to include that will make sense in a story.

Once upon a time, there was a little _____ named Swimmy. The little _____ was very lonely. He didn't have any _____ . Then, the little _____ met a turtle. The turtle was lonely too. They swam together in the cool blue _____, and they had fun.

Children can illustrate copies of their story. The text should be written on several pages, with one or two sentences per page. The little books could be stapled and sent home to share with family and friends.

Sample First-Grade Lessons

While the kindergarten teacher demonstrates how letter/sound associations work, the first-grade teacher includes other skills as well. He or she might also demonstrate invented spelling strategies:

Say the word slowly. Listen for the sounds. Feel them on your tongue and in your mouth. Write down the letters you think you need.

From *Daily Guided Writing.* Text © Carol Simpson and illustrations © Good Year Books.

First-grade teachers will also want to demonstrate the use of letter lines, similar to a Hangman spelling game, in order to spell big words with several syllables. He or she should stress capitalization and punctuation rules in context. Students can also be shown how text wraps around from one line to the next.

Children in a first-grade classroom have just shared the wonderful experience of watching a caterpillar become a butterfly. Some time before, someone had brought in a jar that contained some grass and a furry caterpillar. The teacher had told the children that they could keep it in the classroom and watch what happened to it. Together, they saw the stages of development and wondered what was happening inside the chrysalis. They watched in awe as their butterfly spread its wings and flew away on a cool, sunny afternoon. This shared experience offers an opportunity for guided writing. The teacher asks the children what they remember from watching the butterfly take form. Students eagerly want to tell what they know. Instead of simply taking dictation and writing down what is said as it is told, the teacher can slow the pace a bit and write *with* the students, asking for their help. The guided writing lesson might go something like this:

Teacher: Let's make a story together. Who can help me write down what we learned from watching our caterpillar? What happened first?

Student: Billy brought in a jar.

Teacher: Very good. Let's write that. Billy, please come up here and write your name. (Billy writes his own name.) Billy made a capital *B* at the beginning of his name. The first letter in a name is always a capital letter. Raise your hand if you start your name with a capital letter. (Everyone should raise a hand.) We don't need to make the other letters capitals. Just the first one. Let's all say the letters in Billy's name. (Class chants letters.) Let's see now. Our sentence is going to say that Billy brought in a jar. What is the next word we need to write?

Student: *Brought.*

Teacher: Good. Help me spell that word. Does *brought* start like another word in our sentence? (Teacher writes seven "letter lines": _ _ _ _ _ _ _.)

Student: I think it starts like Billy's name.

Teacher: You are right! Good job! What letter do we need? (B) Is the word *brought* a person's name? (No) The word *brought* is not a name. It is also not the first word in our sentence. So it does not need to begin with a capital letter. (Teacher writes *b* on first letter line.) What other letters do you think we might need to spell this word?

Student: I think there is a *t*.

Teacher: Is the *t* at the beginning or the end of the word? Say it slowly. Where is the *t* sound?

Student: It comes at the end.

Teacher: Right. I'll write a *t* over here. (Teacher writes *t* on the last letter line.) Say the first sound of our word. Do you hear another letter working with *b* at the beginning?

Student: I think it's an *r*.

Teacher: That's right! Good listening! The *r* works with the *b* to say "br" and that letter goes right here. (Teacher writes the letter *r* in its place on the second line.) There are some other letters in the word *brought* that you probably can't hear or feel with your tongue. This word has a funny spelling. It doesn't look the way it sounds. Let me fill in the missing letters. (Teacher continues to spell the word correctly.) Let's read our sentence to find out what is next. So far we have "Billy brought." What else do we want to say?

Student: Billy brought in a jar.

Teacher: Our next word is *in*. Can someone spell that word?

Student: I know how to spell *in*.

Teacher: Can you come up and write the word for us? It goes right here. (Teacher points out the space and student is given the marker to write the word.) Let's be sure not to crowd our letters together. We leave room after *brought* so we can see where *in* begins and ends. We always space our words.

Student: I know how to spell the word *a*.

Teacher: Good. You can come up and write it for us. (Student takes a turn writing.) What is the last word in our sentence? We have "Billy brought in a . . . ." What is next?

Student: *Jar*. Billy brought in a jar.

Teacher: Good. Let's write *jar*. Can anyone tell me a letter that we might need?

Student: I think we need *g*.

Teacher: You might think there is a *g*, but we need a letter that sounds just like *g*.

Student: Is it *j*?

Teacher: Yes. Good for you. We need a *j*. (Teacher writes the letter.) Is there another letter you can hear in the word *jar*?

Student: Is it *r*?

Teacher: Good listening. Yes. It is an *r*. I'll write it over here and leave space for another letter in between the *j* and *r*. The missing letter is one you might not

From *Daily Guided Writing*. Text © Carol Simpson and illustrations © Good Year Books.

know about. There is a letter that works with *r* to make a special sound. Carl has that special spelling in his name. Carl, what letter sits with *r* in your name? Can you tell us? (Carl tells us the letter *a*.) Thank you, Carl. A and *r* go together to make that special sound in his name and in *jar*. (Teacher writes in the missing letter.) Good for us. We have written a good sentence. What does it say?

Student: It says "Billy brought in a jar."

Teacher: That's right. Let's all read it. (Students read together.) Boys and girls, who knows what I should do when I come to the end of a sentence?

Student: You need to put in a period.

Teacher: Yes. I need to put in a period, or some other kind of stop sign that tells the reader to stop and take a breath now. This sentence tells us something, so we will put a period at the end. If it had asked us something, we would have used a different stop sign.

This guided writing lesson continues until the children have helped the teacher write several sentences. It is not necessary to stop and ask how to spell every single word. Children already know how to spell some of the words. Some words the teacher writes without asking for assistance. High-frequency words should be spelled together. The teacher can ask a child to look on the "word wall"* for help in spelling words. The child can spell the word aloud as the teacher writes it. It is helpful for children to chant the spelling of high-frequency words as often as possible.

The experience story that results from a guided writing lesson will probably not be as long as one that is written from dictation. However, the skills and strategies that are taught during guided writing lessons, and recorded on chart paper, will have real meaning to those children who are ready

* A word wall is a large wall space where words are displayed. A word wall commonly contains the high-frequency words that comprise a high percentage of the words we read. They are often words that are vague and cannot be demonstrated with pictures. Words on the word wall are probably in alphabetical order to make it easier to locate them.

to use what has been taught in their own written work.

Along with sentences that tell who brought in the caterpillar, the teacher can ask for, and write with help, other things the students remember from their experience. Here is how another sentence might be demonstrated:

Teacher: Lenita, what do you remember about the butterfly?

Lenita: I remember that it had pretty wings.

Teacher: Help me write that on our paper. Lenita, can you come up here and write your name for me, please? (Lenita writes her name on the paper in the proper place.)

Teacher: We want to say that "Lenita said" something. We need the word *said.* This is a word I want you all to learn to spell. I'll write it down and you can say the letters with me. (Teacher writes *said,* and children chant the letters with her several times.)

Teacher: Help me write what Lenita said about the butterfly's wings.

Student: She said that the butterfly had pretty wings.

Teacher: The butterfly had pretty wings. (Teacher can write Lenita's sentence with or without help, as time permits.) Boys and girls, there is something special about this sentence. It tells us something that someone said. What did Lenita say?

Student: "The butterfly had pretty wings."

Teacher: That's right. I want to show you what Lenita said so I will put special marks around her words. They look like birds. They fly at the top of my line of print. They are called quotation marks and they look like this. (Teacher demonstrates quotation marks.)

From *Daily Guided Writing.* Text © Carol Simpson and illustrations © Good Year Books.

The lesson continues with the period put in place. Perhaps one or two other students will also have their direct quotes written in the experience story. Each time the quotation marks are used, they should be pointed out to students. The use of quotation marks may be difficult for children to understand, but if the marks are used in the context of written work, their purpose might be easier to grasp.

A final step might be to give the story a title. The teacher can ask for help in spelling "The Butterfly" and can show where to write it at the top of the chart paper. (Another lesson could involve using capital letters when writing a story title.) Before writing the title, the teacher asks if anyone can spell *butterfly*. Can someone spot it in the text of the experience story?

Here is an example of a guided story writing experience that stemmed from a shared "noise": The students in my class were lining up after the recess bell had sounded. The children were waiting quietly to return to their classroom when they heard a very loud noise coming from the cafeteria. One of the children exclaimed, "Wow! That sounded like an elephant!" Instead of returning to our room to continue with the lesson plans I had organized for the day, I told the children that we would return to the classroom and write a story about the sound we had just heard. They looked puzzled but pleased.

We began with a rough draft that I wrote in pencil on plain paper. I prompted my first graders to tell me about the sound we had heard. Yes, it did sound like an elephant. "The Elephant in the Cafeteria" is the name of the story that we wrote together. It took a lot of questioning and several days to complete. We were all proud of our effort when it was finished.

We began our story by discussing where we might find an elephant in our school. The children named many places where we might look in order to find the loud animal, including the bathrooms, the kitchen, the closets, and other locations. I made sure I wrote down each suggestion they made. Each idea had merit and made sense in our story. We looked in every suggested place, but each time, "there was no elephant there." We never did locate an elephant in our school. But we did uncover the mysterious noise. The story ends with the sound being heard again and we discover what it really was.

Everyone went back to the cafeteria. The school's custodian was pulling down the tables for lunch. Suddenly the children heard the elephant sound. They looked and saw the custodian laughing. "Is this your elephant?" he asked.

The noise we had heard was the sound of the lunchroom tables being lowered for lunch by our school custodian, Mr. Johnson.

The process of revising and editing our story to make it ready for publication took several days. The story was written on large chart paper and read aloud. Students suggested

changes that needed to be made in order for the story to flow in a logical sequence. The changes were indicated in red. A revised story was again written on chart paper and read aloud. The students still noted minor revisions to be made. They were indicated in red on the second copy. The third revision was accepted by the students as ready for illustration and publication.

The resulting story was cut into chunks so that one or two students could illustrate each page. The children knew which chunk was theirs, and they talked about what should be in their picture. We talked about the color of the elephant, so that everyone who had to draw an elephant would color it the same.

This experience story became a "bound" book that each member of the class (and the school custodian) got to read and share with family and friends. The four days of writing and revising was time well spent.

I included a "Comments" page at the end of the story. This page gives friends and families a place to write their thoughts about our book. A member of the school staff wrote, "Very well illustrated. Enjoyed very much. The sounds are not always what we think." A parent wrote, "I loved the surprise ending!" The children delight in finding out what their readers think of their stories. I always include a "Comments" page in every book that goes out of the classroom. Whether it is going home for an overnight visit or to the school library for a few weeks, it is nice to get reactions from everyone who picks up the book.

The lessons that the children learned from writing "The Elephant in the Cafeteria" were many. They learned about revising and sequencing a story. They learned about editing for proper conventions of print. They saw the rough draft as well as two follow-up versions full of red marks and lines through the words. They learned firsthand about changing the words in the story so that it makes more sense. They also learned an important lesson about their world: They learned to stop and listen and see what is happening around them and to ask questions about it. They learned that "Life is a story. Write about it!" On many occasions after the elephant story-writing experience, I would overhear a child saying, "Now, that's a story!" after hearing or seeing something unusual or new. I enjoyed reading the many stories from real life in their journals.

Sample Second-Grade Lessons

T he experience story that is written by students in a second-grade classroom along with their teacher will be more detailed than those written by either the kindergarten or first-grade groups. Second-grade stories offer opportunities to focus on proper spelling, good sentence structure, paragraph writing, punctuation, capitalization, and other writing skills. They also offer the opportunity to demonstrate editing and revising text. When students have ownership of the words, they are more willing to revise and edit until it makes sense. A classroom that has just shared in the experience of a history unit dealing with Abraham Lincoln might be involved in the following shared writing experience:

Teacher: We have just finished a unit about a very important person in our history, Abraham Lincoln. We have learned a lot about the man and what happened to him. Help me write a few paragraphs that tell some of the important things we want to remember. Let's see if we can write a three-paragraph story. We need a paragraph about his boyhood, one about his political life, and one about his death. What do you think we need to say in our story?

Student: He got shot and he died.

Teacher: Is that something that happened to him early in his life?

Student: No. That's just how he died.

Teacher: We want our paragraphs to tell the story of Lincoln in the right sequence. Should we begin with the way he died? (No.) How might we begin our story? Let's think of something that happened early in his life.

Student: He lived in a log cabin.

Teacher: Good. That is something that happened early in his life. Will you come up here and write that for us?

As students come up to the chart paper, they write their sentences with some teacher guidance. They need to focus on writing the three recommended paragraphs, each paragraph having a specific topic. The first paragraph will deal with Lincoln's early life, the second will deal with Lincoln's political background, and the final paragraph will be about his death. When the experience story is finished, the class and the teacher will need to read it and reread it to see if the sentences are in the proper order. There may be revising and editing that needs to be done in red, right on the chart paper. Students in second grade need to see their ideas being changed and improved through revising and editing. The rough draft of the experience story can be filled with red marks that show how words might be changed and how sentence order might be rearranged, as well as other revising that improves the meaning of the story. Even a second copy can require editing. Students need to see that something might be written many times before it is in final form for others to read.

Another opportunity for a guided writing lesson is when a class is writing a story based upon a book or series of books that the children have read or heard. For example, one group of second graders had read or heard a number of versions of "The Three Little Pigs." First the teacher helped the students brainstorm what might happen in their own version of the famous story. The students dictated their ideas as the teacher wrote them down. The next day, the teacher brought a typed copy of their story, displayed it on an overhead projector,

and read it aloud. The students were quite surprised that their story was so choppy. They told the teacher where changes should be made in the text so that it would make more sense and would be written in a proper sequence. The teacher made the changes on the overhead copy as students watched and made their suggestions.

The next day the teacher shared the new version. The students decided that it still wasn't quite what they wanted it to be. The teacher once again had to make changes on the overhead copy and then retype the story. After three tries the children determined that the story was finished and ready to publish. The teacher then broke the text into thought chunks so that each child had a page to illustrate. The students' pages were put together in a bound book that the members of the class could take home and share with family and friends.

The experience taught them a lot about editing and revising. The idea that nice, clean, typed pages would have to be marked with lots of red pen says something to everyone in the class. It makes them much more willing to edit and revise what they write on other assignments. By showing the revising and editing to a classroom of students, rather than to a single child, it helps ease the pain of learning that what we write the first time isn't always perfect. We learn to appreciate the fact that we can write something better a second or third time. This is an important lesson for children to learn, and the earlier they learn it, the easier it will be for them to accept it when their junior high or high school teacher says that a paper needs more work.

The lessons described here take time to do; hopefully, the skills and strategies that are taught during the guided writing process will be reflected in other written work. Generally, those children who are ready for the concepts being taught will make use of them in other situations. The children who are less ready will probably not try to use them yet.

If this or some other kind of guided writing lesson happens with any consistency or regularity, the children who are not ready at the beginning of the experience will still be able to pick up the skills when they are presented at a later time in the school year.

Chapter 2

Using the Daily News

What Is the Daily News?

The daily news is a group of sentences that conveys information from the teacher to a classroom or group of students. The news can also be a way for students to inform one another about things that are important to them. If incorporated into the classroom schedule as a daily teaching tool, the writing and reading of the daily news can become an excellent way to introduce important ideas and concepts. The content and length of the daily news lessons are without limitations. Similarly, the teaching points to be incorporated in the daily news contents are without boundaries. Students and their teachers may be very surprised at the amount of learning that takes place as a result of a guided news writing lesson. Teachers will be pleased to see examples of daily news lessons in their students' writing in other genres. When asked where the child learned to use quotation marks or commas in a series, he or she may very well say that they learned it in the daily news lesson.

What Do I Need to Begin?

The supply requirements for this activity are minimal. You will need the following items:

Paper: If you prefer to write the news on paper each day, you will need a supply of lined 16" x 24" (or larger) chart tablets. Keep a supply on hand, as you may need to use a sheet of paper, or more, every day of the school year.

Markers: Along with the supply of paper, you will want to get colored markers. The smelly ones provide an extra "hook" to get kids excited about taking a turn writing something in the news. Sometimes it takes that little extra enticement to get children involved in taking risks with writing. You will want enough markers so that each sentence is written in its own color.

Counters: If you are going to include the number of the school day in your daily news, you will need to set up some sort of counting system that you can use every day to determine what day of school it is, such as the 47th or 125th. For counters, you might use tongue depressors, straws, or linking cubes. Make sure you have one counter for each school day. Also make sure that you do not rely on these same counters to do your math lessons. The school day count should remain in place at all times. You will probably want to provide containers for your counters. Plastic bags or boxes covered with colorful peel-and-press paper make good places to show off your ones, tens, and hundreds, and also provide a good way to demonstrate place value. You might also want to provide number flashcards to correspond to the number of counters in each container. When we do the daily count, we learn that when we have filled the ones container with nine counters, it is time to add another container (the tens) in order to write a two-digit number to tell us that we now have ten. We learn that each time we collect nine counters, we know that the next one will make another ten to add to our tens container. Ten counters are then combined to become a "ten" bundle. Each day we count bundles and leftovers (ones) to determine what day of school it is.

A typical lesson in counting the school day might sound like this:

Teacher: Yesterday was the 99th day of school. Let's look at our place-value boxes and count the straws that we see here. How many straws are in the tens box? (90) How many straws are in the ones box? (9) Today we need to add one more straw to our count. Which box should we put it in? (Ones.) Now how many ones do we have? (10) Can we put 10 straws in a box? (No.) Why not? (Because 10 is a two-digit number and we can only have straws that represent single-digit numbers in each box.) What will we do with the straw we add today? (We put it with our 9 ones, making another ten. Then we put the new ten in the tens box.) How many tens bundles do we have in our tens box now? (10) Can we have that many? (No.) Why not? (Because 10 is a two-digit number and we can only have straws that represent a single-digit number in each box.) How many straws are in our tens box before we add today's new ten bundle? (90 straws.) If we add another ten, how many will that be? Let's count by tens to find out (10–20–30–40–50–60–70–80–90–*100*) That's right! We have 100 straws now. We need to create a new place-value box for our 100 straws. We'll call it our hundreds box. When I put our hundred bundle in the new box, how many straws will I have left? (None.) When we write today's school day, we will write 1 for the hundreds box because there is one bundle in there, we will write 0 for the tens box because there are no tens, and we will write 0 for the ones box because there are no ones. Where will we put our straw tomorrow? (In the ones box.)

The following day we would talk about writing a 1 for the hundreds bundle, and a 0 for the tens, and 1 for the ones. We will have 0 for our tens box until we have gathered another ten straws in the ones box. It is great to see children grasping the concept of place value from this daily activity. It makes the math lessons on place value much easier. Children have a good understanding of what the numbers, such as 147, mean. Most will be able to say that the 1 means a hundred bundle, the 4 means four tens, and the 7 is for the leftover ones.

Colored Chalk: Some teachers choose to write the daily news on the chalkboard. This is a workable alternative to paper. In order to demonstrate different sentences, it is advisable, however, to keep a supply of different colors of chalk so that each sentence can be written in its own color. One drawback to using the chalkboard for each writing session is that you cannot save the students' work. If you use paper for writing the news each day, you will end up with copies that you can keep and put in portfolios to show parents at conference times. This is especially helpful when it is a single child writing the entire morning message, complete with the child's own invented spelling and punctuation.

A Gathering Place: You will want your students to be able to sit together in a group on the floor during the daily news demonstrations. They will all need to be able to see the newspaper. Students will need to be able to come up to the newspaper and add their words and lines of text. The newspaper can be hung on an easel or fastened to the chalkboard, whichever is more convenient. If you opt to write on the chalkboard with colored chalk, make sure you have a place for students to gather in front of the board, and make sure you do not expect them to reach too high to write.

When Do I Write the News?

Once you have determined that you will use some form of a daily message with your students, you must decide the time of day when you wish to use it. Selecting the time, and then sticking to it, is more important for emergent learners than it is for independent students. Those in kindergarten and first grade will feel more comfortable participating if the daily news is presented at a consistent time. Second graders are not as reliant on consistent schedules and are often more flexible.

Some teachers prefer writing the news the first thing in the morning. They begin each day with the writing and reading of a few sentences that will tell what is going to happen in school that day. The sentences may be written ahead of time, or they may be written with students watching and having input to the content. There are reasons to have sentences ready to read when students enter the room, and there are reasons to demonstrate the writing of the news.

Some teachers prefer to write the news at the end of the day as a reminder of what was accomplished in the day's work. In this case, it is of great importance to allow for student input. It is very similar to the experience stories discussed previously. The news that is written at the end of the day is written from the standpoint of a shared experience. It may be dictated to the teacher in kindergarten and early first grade and then read and shared. The news that is written at the end of the day can be student-written in the later part of first grade and most of second grade. The teacher can determine who writes the end-of-the-day news and how much content and writing proficiency is expected.

What Can I Teach by Using the Daily News Format?

You as the teacher need to train yourself to look for lessons or teaching points within the daily news lesson. Here are some sample newspapers and the teaching points you might want to consider based upon the content. Although you will find numerous skills that can be taught within the daily news, you will determine which one or two to select as your focus. Students will only get confused if you try to teach every possible skill in a

From *Daily Guided Writing* Text © Carol Simpson and illustrations © Good Year Books.

newspaper! Focusing on one or two each day and then *repeating* the lessons many times during the coming weeks and months is what will help your students become better writers.

You will need to write lines on the newspaper or on the board, called "letter lines," much like those you would use in a game of Hangman. The number of lines drawn represents the number of letters in the word you are trying to spell. Ask students to say the word slowly, listen to the sounds, and feel them in their mouth. Ask students to name the letters they think will be needed in order to spell the necessary word. As correct letters are named, you or a student will write them on the appropriate lines so that the correct spelling of the word in question is the end result.

Good morning.

Today is Tuesday, October 23rd.

It is the 31st day of school.

At 2:15 we will go to art.

Remember to be polite to others.

Jason said, "I got a new bike."

From *Daily Guided Writing.* Text © Carol Simpson and illustrations © Good Year Books.

Lessons to be taught from this newspaper might include:

- capitalization rules
- punctuation rules, including period, comma, and quotation marks
- the name of the current day and its correct spelling
- the name of the current month and its correct spelling
- how to write digital time
- how to spell the word *said*
- finding the word *day* three times (include To*day* and Tues*day)*
- "-ing" spelling pattern in *morning*
- counting one-, two-, and three-digit numbers as you count the school days
- finding one-syllable words
- finding two-syllable words
- finding a word that has *-oo-* as in *wood*
- finding a word that has *-oo-* as in *pool*
- finding a little word in a big word (such as *to* in *October*)
- distinguishing between compound word *today* and two-syllable words
- looking for different sounds of the letter *o* in numerous words
- spelling the word *remember* on letter lines
- the silent *e* rule in *polite* or *bike*
- two *ll*s make just one sound in *will*
- the *-ar-* spelling pattern and sound (*art, farm, party,* etc.)
- the *-or-* spelling pattern and sound (*morning, story, corn,* etc.)
- ordinal numbers (23rd, 31st)

If you look closely at this example, you can probably see other teaching points that you might want to include. If you work with kindergartners or emerging first graders, you can also look for specific letters in each line of the newspaper and circle them with colorful smelly markers. You can ask students to find a word that begins the same as another word, therefore asking them to identify a letter sound and associate that sound with another word. An example is to find a word that starts like *baby* (*bike*). What letter stands for the sound heard at the beginning of both words? Find a word that starts like your name. Find a word that ends like *cat.* The letter/sound lessons are many and will depend upon the level of the students.

Here is yet another newspaper sample. Although many of the teaching points are the same as in the previous example, the minor differences between this newspaper and the one before it make great teaching points that you may not have noticed. A primary difference is the way text flows to a second line rather than having a sentence on each line. *Remember*

that it pays to reinforce what you want children to learn. It will show up in their daily work if you are consistent. As you write, remember to talk about words you want the children to learn quickly. Point out the unusual or unique spelling patterns that need attention.

Good morning. Today is
Wednesday, February 4th. It
is the 100th day of school! We
will celebrate this special day
in many ways. Jennifer said,
"I brought my marble collection."

Lessons you might teach from this newspaper include:

- ◎ capitalization
- ◎ punctuation (period, comma, exclamation point, quotation marks)
- ◎ days of the week
- ◎ months of the year
- ◎ place value, and one-, two-, and three-digit numbers
- ◎ wraparound sentences (a sentence is finished on the NEXT line)
- ◎ ordinal numbers
- ◎ *c* with an *s* sound in *celebration*
- ◎ *c* with a *k* sound in *collection*
- ◎ *day* repeated four times
- ◎ a word that rhymes with *day/s* (*ways*)
- ◎ *y* that sounds like *e* in *many*
- ◎ *y* that sounds like *I* in *my*
- ◎ *-ay* spelling pattern (*day, play, may, way*, etc.)
- ◎ *-ought* spelling pattern (*brought, bought*, etc.)
- ◎ *-tion* spelling pattern (*celebration, vacation, election*, etc.)
- ◎ the spelling of *collection* and *celebration* taught on letter lines

The *ought* and *tion* teaching points are probably more suited to second-grade students and beyond, rather than children in first grade or kindergarten.

Try a daily news lesson similar to this to teach lessons you might not have thought you could do in a newspaper.

Good morning. Today is Monday, April 16th. It is the 149th day of school. What did you do this weekend? Mrs. Johnson will teach us a new song in music. Andy said, "My mom's having a baby on Christmas."

Lessons to be taught from this newspaper might include:
- capitalization
- punctuation
- wraparound writing from line to line
- three-digit numerals and place value
- ordinal numbers
- title/abbreviations: Mrs.
- *mom's,* contraction for "Mom is"
- *-ing* spelling pattern in which the silent *e* must be dropped (*having*)
- *y* as an *e* or *I* in *Andy* and *baby* and *my*
- rule about two vowels (*teach*)
- capitalization of holiday words (*Christmas*)

What Do I Do with the Newspapers?

Space always seems to be a problem in a classroom. There is never enough of it. However, for these lessons you need to collect yet one more thing besides the margarine tubs, sheets of packing bubbles, packing kernels, the meat trays, and all the other items that you just can't do without: you need to collect your daily newspapers as well.

Remember that you will be getting some excellent examples of the children's ability to use letter/sound associations in their invented spelling. You will also see their ability to write independently, not a copying assignment.

I have collected the daily news lessons on chart paper and stapled them together in sets, first by the week, and then a collection of four weeks, which is usually about a month. The children love to look back at the newspapers and read them during their silent reading time. The text is predictable, which is helpful to the emergent reader. The children enjoy reading each other's bits of information in the last line, and will, of course, enjoy reading their own words. When looking at the words and sentences they remember writing themselves, children are able to take note of how much progress they have made in writing independently. They will notice how they used to spell words "when they were little." It's fun to watch them laugh softly at their own mistakes. They really grow a lot when they have guided writing lessons every day.

I suggested stapling the pages together by the week and then putting together monthly sets. You can also put cardboard covers on these sets to make them more stable when they are carried about the classroom. Save the front and back of your chart tablets and use them as covers. You might want to use metal binding rings or colorful plastic "chicken rings" to hold the pages together. If you have access to one, use a spiral binding machine to put the pages and covers together.

If you save your newspapers, you can refer to them often. You can show them to parents at conference time. You will have newspapers from the beginning of the year all the way to the end of the year. The child who has written a bit of news in the last line will have signed his or her name to that sentence, which makes it easy to select and show. As you will read in "Ten Stages of Writing the Daily News" (page 26), during the last quarter of first grade, from mid-March to the end of the year, the children are responsible for doing the entire newspaper by themselves. These full-page writing samples make excellent parent/teacher conference material.

The Kindergarten Newspaper

Kindergarten newspapers are short. They contain only a few sentences, each one written on a separate line of the paper in a different marker color. As is true for any age group, the teacher needs to know the abilities and level of readiness of the students in the classroom. With this in mind, kindergarten teachers may not want to begin lessons in writing the daily newspaper until the second quarter. At this time students may have a better understanding of letter/sound relationships and have had some experience with the alphabet. Also, students will be able to sit attentively as a short message is written. The message may say only:

Good morning.

It is sunny today.

Tasha said, "My dog had puppies."

As the sentences are written, the teacher asks about letter sounds: "What letter do I write to begin/end the word ——-?" Students need to be told about spacing between the words and how the letters sit on the lines. At this time it may be appropriate to talk about the period that tells readers when to take a breath.

An example of a daily news writing lesson might sound like this:

Teacher: I want everyone to look at the newspaper I have started to write this morning. It says, "Good morning." Look where I started my sentence. I started here, on this side of the paper, and I will move this way as I write more words. (Teacher points out left-to-right flow of words.) Who knows which word is *good*?

Student: (pointing) That one. It starts with *g*.

Teacher: Right! What is my other word? (*Morning.*) Boys and girls, take a look at the space I left in between the words *good* and *morning*. I left all of that space for a very good reason. When people write, they have to let the reader know where one word ends and the next one begins. They do this by leaving space between the words, like this. (Teacher might demonstrate by putting two fingers in the space.) In the news I want to say that we will have our school pictures taken today. Here is the word *we*. Let's say the letters of that word. (Students/teacher chant *w-e*.) I put a capital letter at the beginning of the word *We* because it is the first word in the new sentence, "We will have our school pictures taken today."

The teacher writes the new sentence, pointing out the *-oo-* spelling pattern in the word *school*. This is something that many students pick up on early. It is like the word *good* and needs to be singled out. Students might be asked to count the number of words in the long sentence.

The last line of the news would be something dictated by a child.

Teacher: Who has something special to tell us today?

Student: I got a new bike yesterday. I can ride it too!

Teacher: That's wonderful, Billy. What color is your new bike?

Student: It's red and it has a black seat and black tires.

Teacher: How can we put that in a sentence for our news?

Student: I want it to say that my new bike is red.

Teacher: Billy, please come up here and take a marker and write your name for us. (Billy writes his name in the appropriate place on the newspaper.) Let's say the letters in Billy's name. (Everyone chants.) Look at the first letter in Billy's name. It is a capital letter. Does anyone else write a capital letter in their name? (All should raise their hands.) Are all of the letters in Billy's name written in capital letters? (No.) Only the first letter is a capital. Boys and girls, I want you to write your own name like Billy just did, with just one capital letter at the beginning, and the rest are lower-case letters.

The teacher proceeds to write the sentence that Billy dictated, adding quotation marks but probably not mentioning them at the kindergarten level. It is doubtful that students at this age are ready for the concept. The teacher might ask someone to come up and point to the word *bike* in the sentence and then ask how he or she knew that it was the right word. Hopefully, the child will explain that it begins with *b* and that is how *bike* begins. If appropriate for the children, the teacher might also ask about the letter *k* in the word.

When the lesson is done, you might read the red sentence again. You might look at the words in the green sentence to find and circle one that tells someone's name. You might look at the orange sentence to find and underline the word *school* or another important word that you want students to remember.

Remember that your daily kindergarten newspaper can be used to introduce a lot of print concepts that will be further developed in the other elementary grades. Most children who have been introduced to these concepts at an early age, and then revisited with regularity, will not have as much difficulty applying them, when required, later on in school.

The First-Grade Newspaper

A guided news writing lesson should be part of the daily first-grade routine. When a first-grade teacher begins doing a daily news lesson, it should be a very simple message that will probably be written by the teacher without student input. It will be a basic message that will be followed throughout the year, with minor modifications. Some first graders will take note of the message and try to read it. Others will not notice that something is written on the big chart paper. It is important to proceed through some very specific stages of writing development with your group or classroom. The stages should flow smoothly from one to another; each stage adds another important strategy that students need to know. The following ten stages work very well with first graders.

Ten Stages of Writing the Daily News

1. Beginning of the Year (1–2 weeks)

Write the entire message and demonstrate how to spell some of the frequently used words that will be written each day. The length of the news will be very short. Try to keep it to two to three lines plus one child's news (the last line—the "Jamie said . . ." line), which is dictated. If it is a lengthy thought, condense it into a few words. Each line of the news will have its own marker color (or chalk, if using the board). Using different colors for each line is important at this stage because it makes it easy to identify each sentence. "Look at the red line," or "Let's read the blue line" can eventually become, "Jane, you read the green sen-

From *Daily Guided Writing.* Text © Carol Simpson and illustrations © Good Year Books.

tence, and Susan will read the brown one." Each sentence will have its own line of print. The text does not wrap around from line to line. An example of the daily news is:

Good morning.
Today is Tuesday, September 4th.
It is the 7th day of school.
Megan said, "I went to a picnic."

2. Students Fill in the Blanks (2 weeks)

In this stage of development, ask individual students to write in the word that names the day of the week, the month, and the number of the school day. Here is an example of a daily newspaper that contains blank spaces:

Good morning.
Today is _____, _____ 14th.
It is the _____ day of school.

You may want to provide flashcards that contain the names of the days of the week and months to help students correctly write this information in the blank spaces. I provided the names of the school days (*Monday* through *Friday)* on separate cards. I asked the student which card said *Thursday* or the appropriate day. He or she would identify the word card and bring it to the message area to use as a model. I always kept the month names in another area, displaying the name of the current month next to the message area. I changed the month name when a new month arrived. At that time, I put the "old" card back in its place and selected the "new" month card. The display of the school day count was in a nearby location, maintained using containers (ones, tens, and hundreds) with straws. Each day I add another counter and note a new number in the news.

During stage two, you will still be demonstrating and teaching appropriate spelling and punctuation rules consistently as they are being used in context. The students gradually take over the writing of the words. Continue to use multiple marker colors and put one sentence on each line of paper.

3. Changes in the Student's News (By the End of the First Several Weeks)

The difference between stage two and stage three is that the student gets to write his or her own name along with the word *said* in the last line of news. You complete the writing of the child's bit of dictated news and then read it aloud. Determine when your students are ready for this change. It can go hand-in-hand with stage two, just as soon as students have experiences writing in the day, the month, and the school day count a few times.

As you demonstrate the newspaper writing each day, it is important to teach spelling and punctuation lessons continually and reinforce them as they happen in the context of the news. Continue to use multiple colors and single sentences on each line of text.

4. Students Begin to Write More (Two Weeks Before the End of the First Quarter)

At this stage, students will begin to write the "Good morning" and "Today is . . ." lines. With guidance, students are reminded how to spell *Good* (including the capital letter at the beginning of the sentence) because they have seen it every day. The teacher has also noted the *oo* spelling pattern on a regular basis. The *or* after the beginning sound, and the *-ing* at the end of *morning* would also be the subject of continuing discussion as the newspaper is written each day. As the children try to spell the words they are writing, remind them to say the words and listen and feel the sounds in their mouths and with their tongues. "What letters do you think we need?" should be a frequently asked question. Be prepared to make letter lines, either right on the message paper or on a separate piece of paper or on the board, in order to help students spell words such as *morning* (m _ _ _ _ _ _).

As the sounds and letters are suggested, write them in their correct places on the letter lines to show the proper spelling of the word. Allow the student to copy the word in its correct form. This type of spelling by sound demonstration is a valuable method for students to see and learn. It should help them become independent spellers when they write in their journals and in other genres. They learn how to say words and hear and feel sounds that the words contain. Demonstrate the process regularly, using different words in the lesson. Be ready to demonstrate these letter/sound spelling techniques on a daily basis. Sometimes this lesson will be demonstrated using words in the child's bit of news. The words you select to use for demonstration will vary. Be flexible. Repeat spelling demonstrations with frequently used words so that most, if not all, of the children learn how to spell *said* and *good* and *morning* and *today* successfully and as quickly as possible.

From *Daily Guided Writing*. Text © Carol Simpson and illustrations © Good Year Books.

Here is an example of a first-grade newspaper in this stage of development:

Good morning

Today is Friday, October 17th.

It is the 38th day of scool.

John said, "We saw a big cat."

5. Sentences Wraparound (By the End of the First Quarter)

In stage five the teacher will still use numerous marker or chalk colors, one for each sentence in the news. Students will begin to discover that there is still room on the paper to write more words in a line of text. In our classroom reading materials, a new sentence can start where the old one ends. This change begins to show up in our newspaper writing as well. Point out that Laura left us some room after writing "Good morning" and that we can and should make use of the rest of that line on the paper. Change the marker colors for each new sentence, but continue to write in the remaining space that the previous student left you. Point out that the next person will probably have to put some of his or her sentence on a new line because their words may not all fit on a single line of the paper.

Students are learning how text wraps around from line to line. Continue to demonstrate letter/sound spelling using letter lines, when appropriate. Point out capital letters and punctuation marks and talk about the rules for their use. This daily newspaper is an example of how students write in this stage of development.

Good morning. Today is

Monday, November 13.

We will go to music. It is

the 65th dag fol scoohool.

Joseph said, "I'm going to Chicago

on Friday."

These first five stages should take up no more than two months of your valuable time. You will have demonstrated enough of your expectations that students should feel comfortable moving on to the next stage.

6. Students Write Their Own News in the Last Line (Early in the Second Quarter)

Up to this point, you have been writing the last line from dictation as the student tells his or her bit of news. It is now time for the student to write his or her own name, including the word *said,* and then try to write their news, using invented spelling with the letter/sound skills that have been demonstrated each day. The student can do this independently, if you choose, or he or she can ask a friend to help. The student can read aloud what he or she has written when the message is finished. The rest of the class can be talking about other events of the day for the few minutes the student needs to write his or her news. They do not need to watch or participate in the spelling of the words. Each student will have his or her own turn at writing the news.

It takes time to go through this stage. Everyone should have at least one turn at doing this task. Continue using multiple marker or chalk colors for the sentences. Highlight important spelling patterns and frequently used words, as well as punctuation and the use of capital letters.

Here is an example of what was done at this stage.

Good morninig. Toda is Thursday,
December 3rd. We go to
libraryAt 2:45. Today is the 68th
day of soheL. Nadine said, "I
sal Nakke at the srr."

7. Students Are on Their Own (Beginning of Second Semester)

Assign the individual lines of the news when the writing session begins. For example, five first graders wrote these lines:

Good morning. Today is
Wednesday, February 6th.
It is 83rd day School. Will we go to
Library or music? "I got a new
Whatch," siad Megan.

From *Daily Guided Writing.* Text © Carol Simpson and illustrations © Good Year Books.

The students responsible for writing each line will come up, in turn, and do their parts. The rest of the class might be engaged in listening to a story or singing a song. They will not necessarily be watching what is being written. When the news is all finished, ask those who have written the lines to read them aloud. Then look for things that the writer did correctly, such as obvious punctuation and capitalization. Point out correct spellings of frequently used words and close approximations of other words that children try to write. Ask members of the audience if they see any words that they think might be spelled correctly or incorrectly. Demonstrate spelling using letter/sound relationships with letter lines to see if the child has or has not spelled the word correctly. A close approximation is to be commended, especially if the word is difficult! This stage of writing can take a couple of months. It is important that each child has multiple opportunities to write his or her words and thoughts in the newspaper.

8. One Color/One Newspaper (Just Prior to the Last Quarter)

During this stage, a selected group of students use a single marker color throughout the daily news. Each of four or five students will write a specific part of the message. They pass the marker among themselves until the work is finished. Because the news is done in a single color, this is a good opportunity to point out that punctuation marks help us find where sentences end. Periods and question marks will become more important at this stage. The teacher will frequently ask the children how many sentences they see in the newspaper during this stage. Take note of students that might be counting lines of text as opposed to punctuation marks. They can no longer rely on multiple colors to determine how many sentences there are. Remember to continue to ask about words that the children think are spelled correctly/incorrectly. Demonstrate correct spellings with letter lines whenever a good opportunity presents itself.

9. One Student/ One Newspaper (Up to the Final Two Weeks)

During stage nine, students take a giant step. One student writes the entire newspaper in his or her own words using his or her own ideas and thoughts. A single marker color should be used. Students include any information they think is important to share. *The news can become a great creative writing experience at this point.* Take note of students that make changes in the sentence format that has been demonstrated for such a long time. Note who takes risks and tries to spell new words. Note also those who try to write questions rather than all telling sentences. As the student is writing news, the rest of the class can be engaged in a story or song or some other language activity. Ask the student who writes the news to read it aloud and share what he or she thinks is important that day. Here is an example of a single first grader's newspaper:

Good morning. Today is Wednesday, May 5. It is the 156st day of school. "Me and my mom and Gwen and my dad went to The famley Table last nigte and me and my dad sheaired a bnnea spit and we ate it all." Nikki said.

When Nikki finished her writing and sharing, we looked for positive things to say about what she had written. We liked her long, interesting sentence about her experience at the restaurant. We also liked how she used punctuation and capital letters. The children thought Nikki used all of the space on the page.

From *Daily Guided Writing*. Text © Carol Simpson and illustrations © Good Year Books.

If appropriate, we might take time to look at some of the words, such as "bnnea spit," for a lesson in letter/sound spelling. Again, it is important to praise correct spelling and encourage close approximation in invented spelling. Note the close approximation of the words *sheaired* and *nigte* in this example. Encourage students to try to write whatever it is they want to say. They must not feel that they should write only the words that they know they can spell correctly.

Remember: If you use paper each day, rather than chalk on the board, you can save these writing samples to show to parents. Stage nine, the independent stage of news writing, offers a good example of what the child can or cannot do on his or her own when trying to write a message everyone will want to read and hear.

When the child finishes his or her task, he or she reads it aloud and the class looks for compliments to offer. "You did the right thing when you put a capital letter at the beginning of your sentences" or "I like the way you tried to spell the word *school*" (if it is a close approximation). Try to find as many complimentary comments to make as possible. Let the student know that his or her work had a lot of positive points.

It is important to establish a supportive tone in the classroom so that students will not be hurt by having mistakes pointed out. Establish that inappropriate responses will not be tolerated. Begin by asking the class where they think the writer may have used the wrong punctuation. Did he or she place the quotation marks in their proper places in the final sentence? You are demonstrating proofreading and editing skills and are also modeling and teaching students how to make comments in a kind and appropriate manner. Use a different marker color to demonstrate corrections.

At this stage of development, provide an opportunity for each child to write an entire newspaper on his or her own. If there is time, have each child do the newspaper a second time. It does take a great deal of time, but the results are often very demonstrative of the child's independent ability.

10. Editing and Making Corrections (Last Two Weeks of School)

Once again you take over the responsibility of writing the daily news. Prepare the newspaper before the children arrive. It should contain many mistakes, such as the following:

- ☺ misspelled high-frequency words
- ☺ omitted or misplaced punctuation marks
- ☺ omitted or misplaced capital letters

The students proofread the newspaper and find as many mistakes as possible. Tell the children that you and they are looking for 22 (or whatever the number) mistakes today. Can they find all of them? Edit errors in a bright-colored marker or chalk. The students find it a real challenge; they enjoy the hunt.

Here is an example:

Gud mornig boys and grls. Today si Tuesday may 19.
iT iS the 168th day of sckoole we will go ot Art at 2,15
ths aftrnoon. Mrs. Simpson siad, I think "it wil rain"

I am continually surprised at the language skills that I see first graders using in their writing in other areas of the curriculum. When I ask where they learned how to use the skills, the children often say that they saw it in the daily news. There is a definite carryover into other areas of the curriculum.

As a Title 1 teacher in a first-grade pull-out program, I worked with the daily news in yet another format. Two other Title 1 teachers and I had a group of 15 children whom we taught together for one hour every morning. We instructed the whole group in guided writing using the daily news lesson. During the first quarter, we demonstrated all of the writing in front of the whole group. Gradually our students, who were struggling readers, took over the responsibility of writing the message. We decided that our students needed extra practice in writing their "Jamie said" lines and would benefit from that experience at least once a week or more. We would write the greeting, the date, and the school day count together. Then, instead of having one student write his "John said" line on the newspaper, we would divide the chalkboard space into four equal spaces and draw several writing lines in each space. Four students would be selected to go to the board to write their own news lines to share with everyone. It gave our group of struggling readers/writers the extra practice that we felt they needed. Working with this group of 15 students in guided writing, four mornings per week, meant that each child had the opportunity to write news lines once a week. The fifth day of the week was spent in the computer lab, where we often wrote our messages and then printed them. The two other Title 1 teachers and I were pleased with the progress we observed in our children. We hope that what they learned will carry over into the following years of school.

The above described stages seem to fit very neatly in the first-grade experience. Most of the children in kindergarten are not yet ready to write what we are expecting of them in the daily newspaper. They are just beginning to experiment with letters and sounds. Second graders are usually at a more independent stage of learning and are not so reliant upon the gradual initiation of the conventions of the English language that are modeled in the ten stages. My own personal experience has shown me that there is merit in incorporating the ten stages with emergent readers and writers.

The Second-Grade Newspaper

At the beginning of the year, the daily news lesson needs to resemble what was done in the middle of the first-grade year in order to review expectations. This is true for both those who had experienced it in first grade and for those who had not had such a daily guided writing lesson the year before. One second-grade class that tried the morning message with me in early October had not been invited to write the daily news prior to that time. Some students had done such morning writing in first grade with me in their Title 1 classes, but many had not had a guided news lesson in first grade. The second-grade classroom teacher asked for some help in guided writing because she thought her students had forgotten how to use capital letters, punctuation marks, and invented spelling. I agreed to do a guided writing lesson for several days with her students so that she could learn the process.

Here is an example of the resulting early second-grade newspaper:

Good morning. Today
is Monday November 25
We are going to Library at
2:05. Emilee said, I" was in the
prayde and doing acrobac's and doing
cortweds and bacflip's."

As each sentence was written by students, we stopped and looked at the work.

Teacher: Tell me something right about the first sentence.

Students responded with the following thoughts:

He spelled *good.*

He put a capital letter at the beginning of his sentence.

He put a period at the end.

I think he spelled *morning* right.

The words had enough space between them.

Compliments from the other lines of the morning message included:

It's right to put a capital *M* on *Monday.* It's a day of the week.

She put a capital *N* on *November* because it's a month.

I like the way Cody wrote the time. He put two dots in 2:05.

I like that Emilee used "birds" (quotation marks) to show what she said.

Students can really be very complimentary when asked. If you demonstrate how to find and explain what is right with the writing during the early part of the school year, the students will follow your lead. They love to participate in this part of the morning newspaper writing experience.

After finding what is right with each sentence, we then ask what is not right. What needs to be corrected? Students found the following errors:

There aren't any commas between Monday and November and between 25 and 1996.

The word *Library* doesn't need to have a capital letter on it.

We looked at the words *prayde* and *acrobac's* and *cortweds* and wondered if they were really spelled correctly. It was decided that it is probably all right that Emilee didn't spell them perfectly because she was trying to write her message by herself and she didn't have a dictionary with her. We praised her for doing a nice job of making the words close enough to the real spelling that we knew what she wanted to say. We said the words slowly and decided that she wrote what we might have written had we been doing that same sentence without a dictionary.

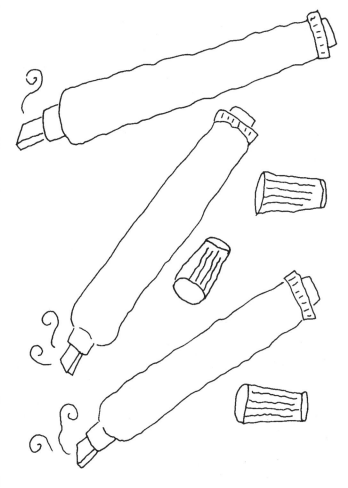

When the work was finished, we also looked at it and thought about how many sentences it contained. (We did use a different color of "smelly" marker for each sentence.) Some students wanted to say that we had written six sentences because that is how many lines we used on the paper. Children who had done morning messages in first grade in Title 1 class were quick to point out that it was four sentences because there were four marker colors. Another child pointed out that there were four periods. A valuable teaching point was presented to the children that we do not put a period at the end of each line of text. A number of children thought it was wrong that there were no periods after *Today, 25, at, the,* and *doing* because these words all appeared at the ends of the lines of text. One of my former first graders, who had done daily news lessons with me, said that we don't put in a period until we are done saying what we want to say. It certainly made my day that one of my Title 1 students would have to explain to his classmates that sentences don't always end just because the writing space has come to an end! I gave myself a quiet pat on the back for spending the time in my first-grade Title 1 classes in teaching guided writing using the daily news. It proved to be worth the time and effort.

As the year progresses, the second-grade newspaper will likely have more sentences and can also be used to introduce topics to be discussed in science and social studies. Depending upon their literacy level, the students may or may not need to see the writing demonstrations done by the teacher for more than the beginning weeks of the school year. It will not be long before the students are involved in the writing of its contents on their own. You may or may not see a need for a student-dictated line of news at this level, although seven-year-olds do like to share their experiences with their classmates. They enjoy bragging about their new bikes or that they went to see a movie or a car race.

A middle-of-the-year second-grade newspaper might say the following:

Good morning boys and girls. Today is Tuesday,
February 10th. It is the 104th day of school.
We will study a map of our state to learn about
rivers, cities, and towns. Do you know where
to find our town on the state map?

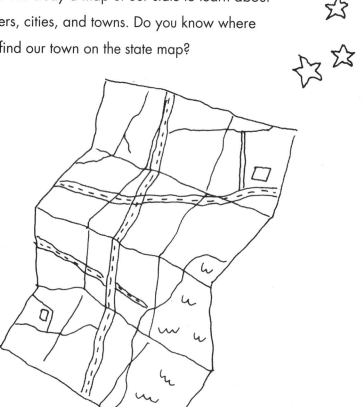

From *Daily Guided Writing*. Text © Carol Simpson and illustrations © Good Year Books.

The teacher wrote the sentences about maps, asking for help in spelling some of the words. Students were asked to write the greeting line, the date, and the school day count. Different marker colors may or may not be used for each sentence at this stage in guided writing. Students and teacher read the news together. Along with the usual letter/sound spelling techniques and other teaching points with this newspaper, the teacher might select a word family to expand upon. The word *map* might lead to a listing of other words in the -*ap* family (*tap, rap, trap, lap, flap, nap, sap, snap,* etc.). An initial look at the state map could also be included as part of the lesson. Commas in a series can be introduced and explained in the context of this newspaper ("rivers, cities, and towns"). Students also look at the message and identify words, punctuation, and capital letters that they think are done correctly.

Teacher: Let's look at Jacob's good morning line. What did he do correctly? Can you compliment him on something in his sentence?

Student: He spaced between the words.

Student: He knows how to put a capital letter at the beginning and a period at the end.

Teacher: What about Judy's sentence about the date?

Student: Judy knows how to spell *Tuesday* and she put a capital letter at the beginning.

Teacher: Good for you. I'm glad you know that those things are done correctly. Can anyone else find something done right?

The compliments can continue as long as interest holds. Students can compliment one another for their neat writing or nice spacing between the words, especially if the writer has many spelling and punctuation errors, which will be discussed afterwards.

The second-grade teacher needs to determine the point at which the morning message and its guided writing demonstration is needed less frequently, perhaps only two or three times a week instead of every day. It may depend upon the kinds of language skills that are being taught in the curriculum. Many, if not most, can be taught in the morning message context. Paragraphing can be taught at the point where second graders are ready for a more detailed newspaper.

By third quarter in the second grade, the teacher might be writing news such as the following, which would be pre-written when students enter:

Today we will be talking about dinosaurs.

There were many kinds of dinosaurs roaming our

earth, and they lived millions of years ago. Some

were very large and fierce and others were smaller

and not so dangerous. Do you know the names of

some of the dinosaurs?

Together the students and the teacher read the message and discuss the ideas presented and the question asked at the end. Selected students are asked to write sentences that answer the question. Here are examples of the resulting sentences that students might try to write in response:

Erin said, "I thik the t-rex was the menest dinosaur."

Martin said, "I like the dinosaurs that culd fly."

Sara "said, I know that dinosaurs are xtint."

First, the class finds ways to compliment each writer. They note the correct punctuation and capitalization. If used correctly, they praise the writers for knowing where to put their quotation marks. After complimenting the writers, the class takes a look at the corrections that need to be made. The teacher selects several teaching points before ending the daily news lesson for the day. Teachers might choose this questioning news option as an alternative to the regular format one day per week. A second day of the week might be the journal critiquing lessons (described in Chapter 3), and the other three days would be the regular format of the daily news, with the typical teaching points included.

Using the questioning technique in the news, the teacher and students read the morning message together and the students respond to the question at that time or some other free time during the day. The statements can then be read and shared at an appropriate follow-up time. Any resulting teaching points are in the context of the students' answers to the weekly question. Since the student responses are written in their own words and at their own ability level, it is possible to look for any misspelled words or incorrectly used punctuation. The students help to proofread and edit everyone's work. Don't forget to also ask for compliments! What did the writer do correctly? The pat on the back is very important in encouraging writers to keep trying.

When second graders become familiar with the format of a daily newspaper and the question/response addition, they can work in small cooperative groups to present their own information. During the final quarter of the school year, the teacher can ask groups of four or five students to work together to write and present to their classmates news from their school, community, state, country, or world. They need to be given adequate time to collect their information and then get it written on a large sheet of lined chart paper. A small group might get their news assignment on Monday and be prepared to present it to the class on Friday. At this point, the 16" x 24" paper will probably not be large enough to accommodate the numerous sentences the students will want and need to write. A 32" x 24" lined tablet might be better for this purpose. The group might need more than one sheet of chart paper. Following is an example of a daily newspaper written by a group of second graders. They used dictionaries to check their spelling.

There will be a reading fair at our school

this week on Thursday at 10:30. Everyone should

bring a book to read. Some parents will come in

and read to us too.

The mall has a new bookstore. Be sure to

go there and look around. They have some neat

books about dinosaurs and monsters.

A hurricane came last Saturday. It knocked

down some houses along the ocean in Virginia. We

are lucky that it didn't come here.

Upon presentation of this newspaper, prepared cooperatively by the group of students, the teacher and audience look for ways to compliment the writers. They identify correct spellings, capitalization, punctuation, neat writing, nice spacing between words, and other correct uses of the English language. Then, students look for misspelled words and any improper punctuation and/or capitalization. They also look at the content of each of the three paragraphs. Is the content consistent with the topic of the paragraph? Any errors would be corrected using a bright-colored marker so that they are readily seen. Teaching points that might result from this student-prepared newspaper include:

- what to include as items of interest in the newspaper
- compound words
- silent *k* followed by *n (knocked)*
- contractions
- paragraphing (each paragraph discusses a different topic)
- nouns and verbs
- adjectives

The teacher who uses the daily/weekly newspaper or message will learn to look for teaching points in every piece of writing that is demonstrated or shared with children.

Journals as Guided Writing Lessons

The teacher who relinquishes precious time each day to allow journal writing will understand the numerous teaching points and writing demonstrations that can be taught based upon anonymous passages written by the students. Once a week— or more often as time permits—collect journals and take time to read the entries. Respond to them right on the journal page as you see fit. Compliment when it is appropriate but also let students know when their writing is too sloppy for you to read. Look for two or three anonymous examples to copy onto chart paper, just as they are written in the journals, complete with all errors. The examples do not need to be lengthy. A sentence or two from two or three journals will be sufficient to demonstrate your teaching points.

What will you want to demonstrate? That will be up to you. You may find an entry in which a student is trying to use quotation marks, but has them in the wrong place. You might look for an example that contains a spelling pattern or phonetic rule you have been studying. For example, if you have been working on the *-tion* spelling pattern and you see a journal entry with the word *vacashun,* you might present the correct way to spell the word, stressing the pattern that you had just taught. Look for examples that have incorrect usage of pronouns, contractions, or compound words. Look for examples with poor sequencing of events, if they can be demonstrated in a few short sentences. As with the news and experience stories, be sure to include compliments as an important part of the lesson. Let the writers know, anonymously if possible, that they did a nice job. Students will usually recognize their own work samples and will give themselves a quiet pat on the back when they are complimented. Do the praising, then do the correcting. Keep in mind that you do not need to show every correction you might want to make with an example. *Two or three suggestions, or even just one, might be enough to stress your important teaching points.*

What About Kindergarten?

There are many kindergarten teachers who allow journal time every day. More often than not, the children are only drawing pictures and not trying to write words in the beginning of the year. You might make a copy of a child's picture and then demonstrate for the group how you might add words to it. If the picture is of a dog, you will want to label it with the word *dog*. Ask children what letter is at the beginning of the word (d). Ask what letter makes the ending sound in the word *dog* (g). You might demonstrate how to write a sentence about the picture. Perhaps you could write:

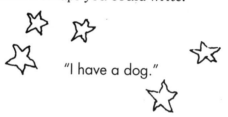

"I have a dog."

As you write, talk about the capital letter at the beginning, the letters and the sounds they make, and the period at the end of the sentence, and the space between the words.

When kindergartners are starting to write some words, look for examples of strings of letters that do or do not make sense. Compliment the child who writes anything that demonstrates an understanding of letter sounds at the beginning of his or her words, as well as the child who writes in a combination of upper-case and lower-case letters. Praise the child whose letters are formed correctly, and who makes sure the letters sit properly on the writing lines. You should also compliment the nice coloring/drawing done by someone who hesitates to write any words yet. Encourage them by showing them what they might write the next time.

From *Daily Guided Writing*. Text © Carol Simpson and illustrations © Good Year Books.

First-Grade Journals

T he beginning days or weeks of the new year will probably bring with it a lot of journals filled with pictures and no words. Encourage your students to include words by demonstrating what they might write to go with their picture, just as with the kindergartners. Those students who are ready to include words will want to try to do so. Look for examples of invented spelling to put on chart paper. Keep the examples anonymous, if you can. Praise the effort and demonstrate how the work was done, and how you want more students to give it a try.

An early example is as follows:

"I S a srsr"

This attempt at writing a sentence accompanied a picture of a star. Kirsten was trying to say, "It is a star." The illustration she included with her sentence provides a lot of help in determining what the text says. Kirsten should be praised for trying to write a sentence about her picture rather than just making a drawing and nothing else.

Teacher: Let's see if we can compliment Kirsten's work.

Student: She wrote a capital *I* at the beginning.

Student: She didn't make the word *a* a capital.

Teacher: Kirsten also did a good job of trying to spell *star*. Here is the correct 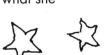 way. Kirsten got the *s* and the *r* right! She did a nice job of writing what she wanted to say.

By first pointing out her strengths, Kirsten will be encouraged to try to write words again. She will not feel defeated when we point out the corrections if we give her an anonymous pat on the back first. Teaching points might include putting a period at the end of her sentence and spelling *It is* because the words are introduced in spelling early in the year. Rather than make all of the needed corrections in Kirsten's work, stress a single teaching point and then go on to a second example. The child doesn't need to hear too many negatives at this stage of development. We want children to try again!

During the first few weeks of school, Megan wrote:

  M G R A M U G U U W O B M L N W P I S W T M L N

This may look like a string of random letters when seen by itself. When combined with the drawing of a person and a plant she had done on the same page, it is easier to understand what the child was trying to say:

 My grandma gots a watermelon. We picked the watermelon.

Megan actually did write many letters that are in the words. She is to be congratulated for getting more than just first letters correct. She also has several syllables represented in her spelling of the word *watermelon*. Megan shows that she knows a lot about letter sounds. Highlighting her work in a guided writing lesson will help her understand that there are other things she might do to become a better writer. Teaching points might include that all of our letters should not be written in their capital form. I might also demonstrate how words need to be spaced so that we can tell where *grandma* and *watermelon* begin and end.

For another example, look at Kyle's sentence:

I Plad wita my Frnd we Plad fres tag

Kyle's effort at inventing his spelling should be praised. The teacher was able to read the example without needing his help. It can also be read without the help of a picture, and Kyle was able to spell four words correctly. The words *plad, wita, Frnd,* and *fres* are easy to read because he said the words slowly and then wrote down the letters he thought he heard. Teaching points to accompany this example might include the fact that we do not need capital letters on the words *Plad* and *Frnd.* Also, that we put a capital letter at the beginning of a sentence and when we write a special word, such as somebody's name. If we read the example slowly, we might determine that the writer was really telling us two things. He has really written two sentences and, therefore needs periods at the end of both sentences.

Invented spelling needs to be encouraged in the context of the students' own work, and it is a very valuable skill for all children to learn. We must not assume that children know how to say a word slowly and listen for letters and sounds. This process needs to be modeled regularly in order for all children to understand the technique. It is also important to point out that perfect spelling is very desirable, but that it is not expected from writers when they are trying to put their thoughts in their journals. Teachers do want to see high-frequency words spelled correctly because they have been introduced in spelling lists or are available on word walls or class dictionaries for correct spelling. Children need to know that it is all right to look at, and copy, a word from the word wall, a chart, or a dictionary, in order to spell the word correctly. Children need to know that they cannot ask how to spell every single word they want to write or they will be wasting time. Moreover their ideas will end up being forgotten while they wait for the teacher's help. Independence in writing is an important goal, and using invented spelling is an important part of becoming independent.

The idea of a child expecting himself or herself to spell every word correctly can stifle writing. Amanda wrote this example in November of first grade:

I go to a bee the bee sting Me

Among the few words introduced in early spelling tests up to this point were *I, go, to, in, is, a, the,* and *me.* Amanda used many of those words because she knew she could spell them correctly. She spelled *bee* from memory, after having seen it in a book she particularly liked. The word *sting* was spelled with help from the teacher. This child needs to be praised for trying to write sentences that make sense and are spelled correctly but she also needs to be shown that there might be a more interesting way of expressing her thoughts. "I saw a bee. It stung me." Teaching points from this example might include the idea that the writer really told us two things in her story. As a group, we can read it carefully and then decide where the first sentence ends and the next one begins and put in periods where needed. A capital letter at the beginning of the second sentence might also be demonstrated in connection with that idea.

Second-Grade Journals

In my experience, most second graders begin their journal writing year by writing sentences. They may or may not draw a picture to accompany their words. The picture is not the focal point as it is in kindergarten and first-grade journal work. I think that selecting anonymous examples for lessons in complimenting and editing is an easier task in second grade than it is in the earlier grades. The majority of students will have tried to write something and most likely have made some errors that you want everyone in the class to see, to help edit, and to explain why or how to correct them.

One common writing problem in second grade is the run-on sentence. Students want to connect everything with "and then," which creates a single long sentence. Select an example that includes three or four "and then" phrases and put the text on chart paper, just as the student wrote it.

Today I want for a wauk with my friend and then we sol a rabbit and then we sol a dog and then we sol a snak.

From *Daily Guided Writing.* Text © Carol Simpson and illustrations © Good Year Books.

This student needs to know that he has written a very interesting "story" about a walk that he took with his friend. We might encourage him to write more about the things he saw on his walk with his friend, and give more details. Perhaps such a story ("My Walk") could be published so that others might get to read and enjoy it. The writer needs to know what he might change before it gets published. Here is an example of a lesson on revising a journal entry.

Teacher: When I read your journals, I found an interesting story about a walk someone took. Here are some of the things that this person wrote. (The teacher writes the example on the chart paper for everyone to see.) Can you compliment the writer about something you think is good?

Student: This person spelled a lot of words right.

Student: This person knows how to put in capital letters and periods.

Student: This person has some good ideas for a story. Maybe it can be published.

Teacher: I was thinking that very same thing. Can we help the writer make it sound better? What if we take out some of the "and then" phrases? How will it sound?

Next, read the story without the "and then" phrases. Does it sound any better? Most will say yes. However, the resulting sentences will sound very short and choppy because of the change. Discuss how the writer might add some other words that make the story more interesting.

Teacher: The writer talks about seeing a rabbit. I wonder if the rabbit was white. I wonder if the rabbit was eating or hopping or doing something interesting. How might we put that in this story? Does it sound OK to say that "We saw a white rabbit hopping across the neighbor's yard"?

Student: That sounds good.

Teacher: The writer might also want to describe the dog and the snake in the same kind of way. I wonder if there was something that happened after their walk. Do you suppose they went back home and shared cookies and milk? I'll bet they were tired after their long walk. The writer might think of a nice way to end this interesting story.

Hopefully, the writer of the passage will revise his journal entry by providing more details and by editing the "and then" phrases. The result will be a story that sounds better, is more interesting to the reader, and is ready for possible publishing.

Another common problem with second graders is that they say they don't know what to write about. This will become less of a problem if the teacher singles out those few interesting passages that make a "story" that the writer tells from personal experience. The passages need not be lengthy; they just need to "tell a story." If students see that the result might be a published book, they will all want to get involved in writing interesting things in their journals. The first few stories that get published will probably be rather short and lack creativity. But give publishing a chance—the stories do get better! A variety of publishing options are included in the Appendix.

A second-grade student, Megan, had written a page of questions in her journal. She was parodying a library book she had read. Her questions all related to colors.

Why are oranges orange?

Why are some cats white?

Why are some dogs brown?

Why are oceans blue?

When these passages were read aloud from the author's chair, Megan was encouraged to continue the established pattern by asking more questions. The audience enjoyed the variety of thoughts she shared. Her final product was published as "The Why Book." Her last page was a nice summary statement. "There are many different colors in the world and I'm glad." Megan did not attempt to answer the questions she had asked in the text. When I conferenced privately with her, she told me that she would know the answers when she goes to college! Her objective was not to answer the questions, but simply to offer food for thought.

Second graders will become more creative when they see the response to their writing from their peers, teachers, and other adults. With practice, they will begin to listen to the world around them and question what they hear. They will begin to realize that "Life is a story. Write about it!" Special events, unusual sounds, or new experiences can become the subject of journal entries. A story prompt is not always necessary.

If you demonstrate the procedure for students, they will become better listeners when writers share their work from the author's chair. They will follow your lead and begin to question each other about their stories. Sometimes the discussion of journal entries helps students come up with new story ideas. It can encourage them to continue with a good story, and it can lead to suggestions on how to end the story or make it more interesting to the audience.

Appendix

This Appendix contains the following pages, some of which can be reproduced, for your use in enhancing students' writing experiences:

- ☺ a daily news fill-in-the-blank page
- ☺ a weekly news summary page
- ☺ options for publishing students' writing
- ☺ writing prompts

Reproducible Daily Newspaper

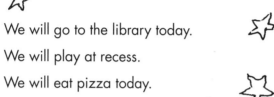

Following is a blackline master with a fill-in-the-blank news outline. It contains a line for the greeting, starting with *Good*. There are lines for the date, the school day count, and for a child's account of something the class will do today. "We will _____" might be finished by saying:

We will go to the library today.

We will play at recess.

We will eat pizza today.

Each child can write his or her own greeting in the space provided. Encourage the children to start with the word *Good* and then complete the sentence with their own words. Children may choose to write the familiar "Good morning." But some students might choose to add other words, such as in the examples below. Be sure to praise those students who show creativity and a willingness to invent their spelling in an attempt to say something new and different. Sample greetings include:

Good morning, everyone.

Good morning, boys and girls.

Good day to all of you.

Students will select their own words for the "____ said" space. They will write their own name in the space before the word *said* and then they will write their own bit of news independently. Try to allow some sharing time so that students who want to can share what they have written in that last line. Some might also want to share their "We will . . ." line as well.

There is space on the blackline master for students to draw pictures that illustrate their bit of news. This drawing is often helpful in determining what the words say. This is especially true with early emergent writers whose invented spelling is just beginning to show signs of development and an understanding of letter/sound associations.

This fill-in-the-blank blackline master provides a good writing sample to put in the child's portfolio to show parents at conference time. It should be dated each time it is written and can be put in sequential order to show the child's progress.

The Daily News

Name _____

Good _____ .

Today is _____ ,

_____ the _____ .

It is the _____ day of school.

We will _____

_____

_____

_____

_____ .

_____ said, "_____

_____ ."

Reproducible Weekly News with Illustrations

The blackline master that follows is appropriate for kindergarten, first grade, and second grade. It offers the opportunity for the child who shared his or her news (the "Jamie said" line) that day another chance to share it and illustrate it for others to see. Either the student or the teacher can write that bit of news in the lines beside the appropriate day of the week at the bottom of the page. The child has a place to draw an accompanying picture at the top of the page in the corresponding day of the week box.

This page should be started on a Monday and filled in each day of school for one week. On Friday, the teacher should make photocopies of this page for everyone to take home. This is especially enjoyable for the children who have a sentence and picture included in the news that week.

All of the original copies of the weekly news reports can be placed in a notebook. Children can select the notebook as reading material during independent reading time. They often enjoy reading the "old" newspaper stories over and over again. Children love finding their own names and rereading their news items.

From *Daily Guided Writing*. Text © Carol Simpson and illustrations © Good Year Books.

Week of _____

Monday _____
_____

Tuesday _____
_____

Wednesday _____
_____

Thursday _____
_____

Friday _____
_____

Publishing Students' Stories

There are many ways to publish students' stories. Most are very inexpensive. Materials and time requirements vary with each technique. If you do not already publish students' writing on a regular basis, and you decide you want to try it, you may be surprised at the results. Once one child publishes a book, whatever the publishing technique, other students usually want to do the same. Encourage your students to try and be creative in their journal writing by rewarding them with publishing their work.

How are stories selected for publishing? In the beginning of the school year, look for very simple story ideas to edit and publish. After the initial ideas have been revised and made more interesting, they are published by having them typed on a computer. A student may be asked to copy his or her story on the pages if a computer is not available. Give students space to draw illustrations to accompany their stories.

Ways to Publish

Metal or Plastic Rings: An easy way to compile pages to make a book is to punch several holes in the manuscript and put metal rings through the holes. The more holes punched, the more stable the pages will be when they are turned. This is a relatively inexpensive way

to publish students' work, and the time it takes to punch the holes and put the pages together is minimal. Metal rings can be purchased at a discount office supply store. For most students' stories, smaller rings work better than the larger sized ones. Be careful when you punch your holes so that you do not punch them too far away from the edge of the pages. Reinforce punched holes with clear packaging tape placed on both the front and back side of the pages before they are punched and bound.

A less expensive alternative to metal rings is to use "chicken rings." These are brightly colored plastic rings that function like the metal ring you use to keep your keys together. They come packaged in large quantities for a very minimal amount of money. Chicken rings can be found in specialized math supplies catalogs. A lot of stories can be published with just one package of chicken rings.

Another way to help the stability of the pages you are binding with rings, regardless of whether you use metal or plastic, is to reinforce the covers with cardboard. Save cardboard pieces from the fronts and backs of chart tablets or collect pieces of cardboard of various sizes from boxes. Cardboard packaging material can also be used.

If cardboard pieces are plain (no printed matter on them) students can write directly on them to create covers. If the cardboard pieces have writing on them, cover them with something such as colorful adhesive peel-and-press paper that comes on rolls.

The Spiral Binding Machine: A spiral binding machine is a very simple machine to use, but expensive to buy initially. Materials needed include plastic binding strips, which are not expensive to keep on hand, and multicolored posterboard-weight paper. The child whose story is being published can select the color of posterboard for their book cover. The child can decorate his or her cover with markers. Space is allowed on each page so students can illustrate their work. (Stories are revised and edited by student and teacher before the book is bound.)

Make a Book by Taping the Pages: The metal and plastic rings and the spiral binding machine are all great for a spur-of-the-moment publishing method. If there is time and a more professional job of binding a really special story is desired, a more sophisticated method of publishing stories is to make a taped book. I wish I could take the credit for this idea, which is really simple to use. It's one of those things you see and you think, "Why didn't I think of that?" It came from a very dear friend, who had gotten the idea from another friend, who had gotten the idea from another source. The originator of this process is "anonymous."

Place the pages of your story upside-down on the table. Take one page at a time, starting from the last page, turning the pages right side up and taping the left edge of the paper to the table or work surface. Use clear packaging tape that is about 2" to 3" wide. Each page is taped where the spine would be, one page on top of the other, to the table or work surface. When you have taped all of the pages, peel the pages off of the table and fold the excess tape behind so that it fastens to the back of the last page. When the pages of this kind of published story are opened, they are nice and flat. The pages don't bunch and are very easy to turn. See the illustration below to help you accomplish this simple task.

Add a book cover that is made of cardboard that has been covered with colorful peel-and-press paper. The illustration shows how to do this. The child whose story is being published can choose the color or design of the cover. To make the cover, use two pieces of cardboard, both the same size as the pages of the story that is being bound. Cut a piece of peel-and-press paper that is more than large enough to place both the front and the back covers on it and still have at least 2" of adhesive paper left to fold over the edges. Peel off the backing and lay the sheet of adhesive paper upside-down on the table (sticky side up). Carefully lay your cardboard pieces in place. Be sure to leave about 1" of space between your two pieces of cardboard when you lay them on the adhesive paper.

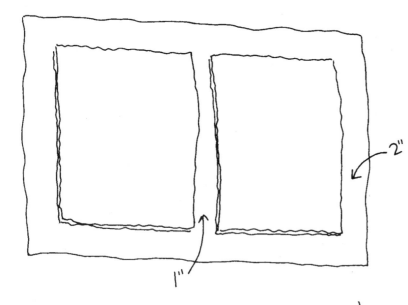

2"

1"

Fold over the excess adhesive paper and press into place to make smooth edges. If desired, cut out the corners before they are folded.

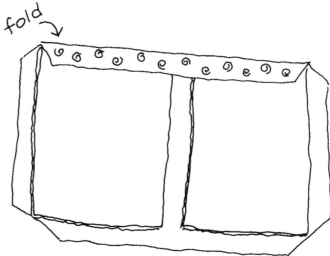

fold

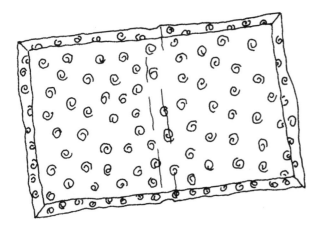

Next, cut another piece of adhesive paper that will fit inside the covers. Cut the paper slightly smaller than the size of the two cardboard cover pieces together. Fasten the adhesive paper to the inside by peeling off the backing and carefully laying it in place.

Next, fasten the taped story pages inside of the cardboard cover. Once again use the clear, wide packaging tape to fasten the pages in place. This time, place the tape in such a way that the excess tape will fasten to the inside of the book. Put tape inside both the front and the back covers. Be sure to place the pages in the center of the cardboard in the 1" space that was allotted for folding the book.

If an ample supply of cardboard is available, prepare a large quantity of ready-made covers. Select two identical sized pieces of cardboard. Cover them with different colors and patterns of peel-and-press paper or wallpaper, remembering to leave the 1" space between the pieces. Keep the covers on hand for publishing "on the spot." If a supply of 8 1/2" x 11" sized covers are available, most of the stories that come out of the classroom can be published quickly, because most will have been written on 8 1/2" x 11" paper. Quickly tape the pages and put them in a ready-made cover.

Make a Book with a Fancy Cardboard Cover: An elaborate cover for a story can be made using peel-and-press paper and heavy cardboard. The steps in this binding process are more complicated and time consuming. The story cannot be printed on a computer because the pages of this story will be folded and center stapled so that each sheet of paper will become four pages of the resulting book. The student author can either elect to print his or her own text on the pages, or the words can be typed and then cut and glued into place on the pages of the book. Start with sheets of blank paper. Legal-sized paper, 8 1/2" x 14", works well. This size of paper, when folded in half, makes a nice little book, approximately 9" x 9" when finished.

First count the number of pages needed for the story. Be sure to add a page for the title, "The End," a dedication page if desired, a page with author information, and a page for comments if the student plans to share his or her story and wants to get feedback from the readers. Divide the number of pages needed by 4 to determine the number of blank sheets of paper required to start the publishing process. If the story is 13 pages, you will need 4 sheets of blank paper. A 27-page book requires 7 sheets. An 8-page book will require only 2 sheets.

Fold and center staple (or sew on a machine in a loose stitch) the blank pages along with a piece of peel-and-press paper with the design side up. The peel-and-press paper needs to be cut to 8 1/2" x 14" just like the blank paper.

Use two pieces of cardboard, 9" x 9". It is important that the two pieces be the same size and type of cardboard. Heavier cardboard, such as that used for boxes, works better than a lighter weight cardboard, such as a tablet backing.

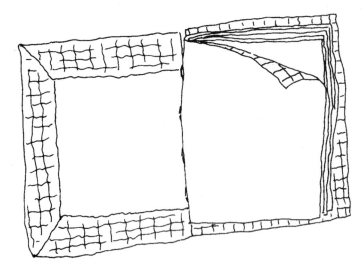

Place the two pieces of cardboard 1" apart and fasten to the sticky side of a large sheet of peel-and-press paper. The peel-and press-paper needs to be at least 12" x 22" in order to cover and fold over the cardboard.

Remove the backing from the peel-and-press paper that is stapled to the blank book pages and press it carefully in place on the inside of the cardboard cover.

The student can then write his or her words on lines that can be drawn in place if desired. Or he or she can type the story and glue the text in its proper place. The child can then draw illustrations to go with the text. The book that results from this lengthy process will be a real treasure to the young author. Other members of the class will want to write their own books! The idea of publishing will catch on quickly when students see the resulting books.

Reproducible
Story Starters

A Better World
The Deep Hole
Chores
Seasonal Changes
Winter Dreams
Mud Puddles
Tracks in the Snow
Monkey Tales
Nobody Saw Me
Followed Home
My Collection
My Favorite Hiding Place
I Was Very Brave
How to Cook a Special Dish
Excuses, Excuses!

A Better World

The following story prompt can be used any time. It might be best to use it after a unit on recycling and/or the environment. The prompt asks students how they can make the world a better place.

Begin by discussing with students environmental and human issues. How in-depth the discussion will be depends on the teacher and students. What are some of the problems we face in this world? How can we work on these problems? As a child, you *can* make a difference. One child can share his or her ideas with another child and another child and another child—helpful ideas will spread. The class can share *The Great Kapok Tree* by Lynn Cherry as an introduction to this writing prompt. *Dear Children of the Earth: A Letter from Home* by Schim Schimmel is another excellent book to share and discuss prior to writing. The illustrations are very thought provoking.

I can help make the world a better place by . . .

From *Daily Guided Writing* Text © Carol Simpson and Illustrations © Good Year Books.

I can help make the world a better place by _____

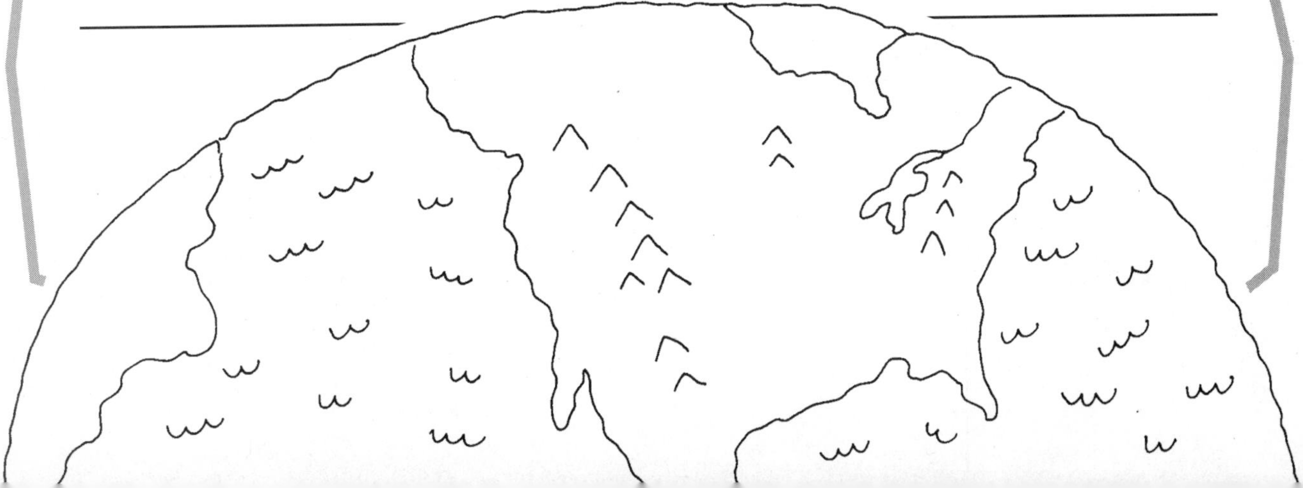

_____

_____

_____

_____

_____

_____

_____

_____

_____

_____

The Deep Hole

The story prompt that follows asks the students to imagine that they have fallen in a deep hole on the school playground. They will write about what happens to them in the hole. You might relate the idea of what happened in the story of *Alice in Wonderland* by Lewis Carroll as a lead-in to this writing experience. Questions you might want students to ask themselves are:

- How did the hole get there?
- How deep is the hole?
- Where did I end up?
- What did I find when I got there?
- How can I get back out?

Students can share their responses to the stories.

I fell into a deep hole on the school playground. It was exciting!

From *Daily Guided Writing*. Text © Carol Simpson and Illustrations © Good Year Books.

I fell into a deep hole on the school playground. It was

exciting! _____

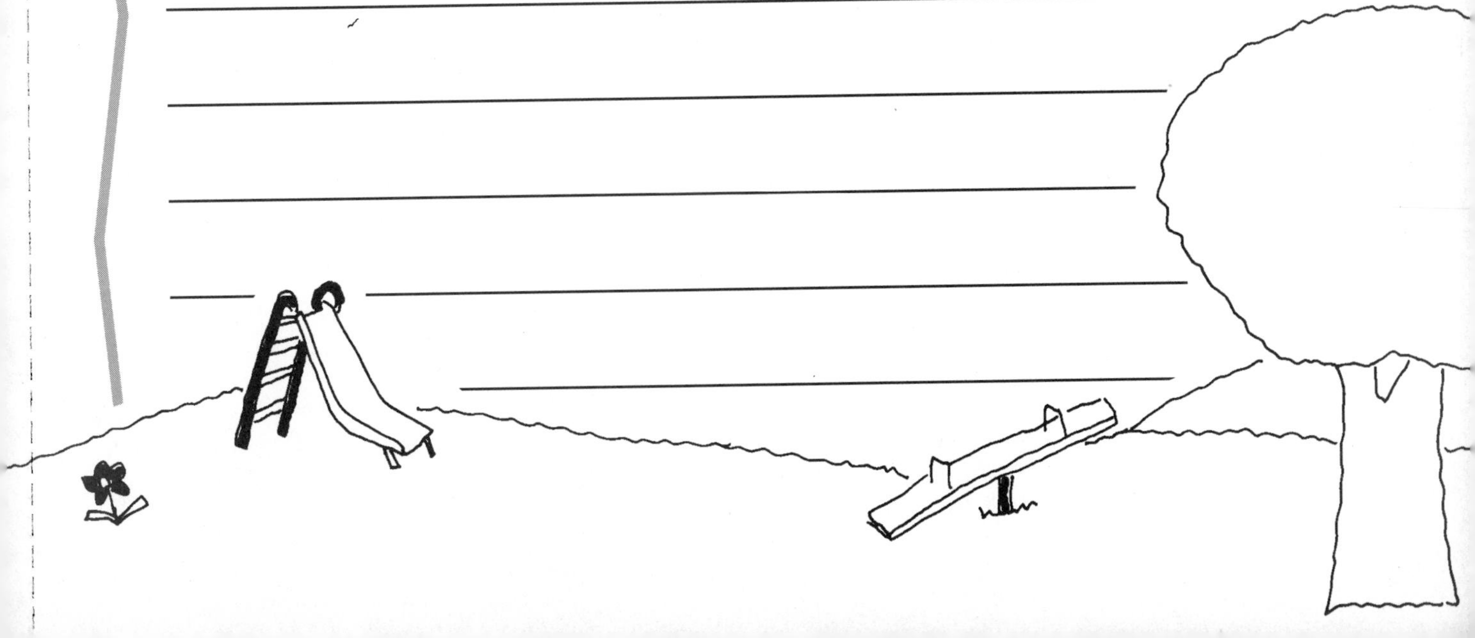

_____

_____

_____

_____

_____

_____

_____

_____

_____

_____

_____

_____

Chores

The purpose of this story prompt is to inspire creative thoughts about chores and animals. Students will be asked to think of a chore that they don't like to do, and then imagine that an animal can do that chore for them. What chore might it be? What animal would they want to help them do the work?

Start by making a list of typical "kid" chores such as doing homework, taking out the trash, or cleaning their room.

Next, ask children to imagine that they could choose an animal to do the work for them, or at least help them to get the job done. Brainstorm a list of animals and what chores they might do. *If the Dinosaurs Came Back* by Bernard Most suggests things dinosaurs might do to help us in this life.

I'm going to get . . . to help me . . . because . . .

From *Daily Guided Writing* Text © Carol Simpson and illustrations © Good Year Books

I'm going to get _____

to help me _____

because _____

_____

_____

_____

_____

_____

_____

_____

_____

_____

Seasonal Changes

Use the following story starter during seasonal changes. Begin with a discussion of the changes that take place in your part of the country when the temperature changes. What happens to animals that leave and go to another place during the cold? What happens to the leaves on the trees when the wind takes them away? Discussions might also include talk about the summer clothes that are put away until the next year. You might talk about the snow and what happens to it when the temperature rises. What happens to the snow boots and sleds when the weather changes? The possibilities for filling in the topic are many. All it takes is a bit of brainstorming to get ideas flowing.

I wonder what has happened to . . . now that the weather has changed.

From *Daily Guided Writing Text* © Carol Simpson and illustrations © Good Year Books.

I wonder what has happened to _____ now

that the weather has changed. _____

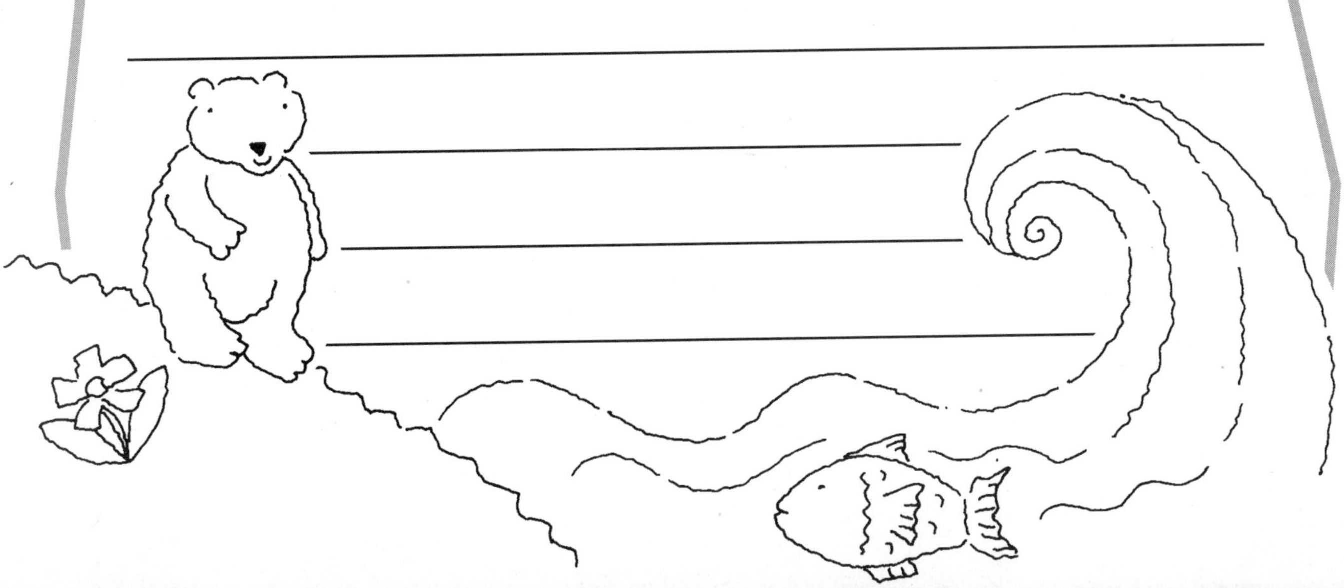

_____

_____

_____

_____

_____

_____

_____

_____

_____

_____

_____

_____

Winter Dreams

The blackline master that follows can be used during cold winter months. A particularly cold and windy day, when children cannot go outside, might inspire some warm thoughts!

Begin by brainstorming a list of all the warm places you would rather be on such a cold day. Suggestions that warm the soul might include an island in the middle of the ocean; Hawaii; a warm, sandy beach; or a heated swimming pool. Encourage children to imagine how they would feel if they could be transported to a warm place instantly. Where would they go and what would they do there?

I am going to snap my fingers and suddenly I'll be in a warm place!

I am going to snap my fingers and suddenly I'll be in a warm place! I'm going to _____ and when I get there, _____

_____

_____

_____

_____

_____

_____

_____

_____

_____

Mud Puddles

I t is finally spring! Together, brainstorm ideas that fit the prompt. Talk about how parents feel if their kids get muddy. Also, talk about how mud feels on a warm day when you walk barefoot through it. Most children will think the experience is fun, even though they may get in trouble for doing it.

Two good poems to read and discuss before writing stories are "The Muddy Puddle" by Dennis Lee and "Mud" by Polly Chase Boyden.

I found a really big mud puddle!

I found a really big mud puddle! I was told not to get dirty, but

I played in it anyway. Here's what happened. _____

_____

_____

_____

_____

_____

_____

_____

_____

_____

_____

_____

_____

Tracks in the Snow

I f your winter happens to involve snow, imagine going outside on a snowy day and finding tracks left by an animal or person. Who might have made the tracks in the snow? What might happen if you follow those tracks? What or who might you find? Where might the tracks take you? You may want to share *The Snowy Day* by Ezra Jack Keats for inspiration.

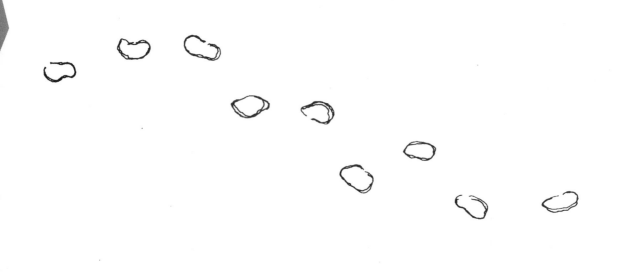

I went outside and found tracks in the snow.

From *Daily Guided Writing*. Text © Carol Simpson and illustrations © Good Year Books

I went outside and found tracks in the snow. What an

adventure I had!_____

_____

_____

_____

_____

_____

_____

_____

_____

_____

_____

_____

Monkey Tales

This prompt deals with cute, but naughty, monkey business. Monkeys are cute little animals. We love to watch them in the zoo. Think, however, of the character Curious George, created by H. A. Rey. Imagine monkeys that are mischievous as well as cute. What might happen if a little monkey did not listen to his mother when she said to stay out of trouble? Where might the little monkey go? What might he do to get into trouble? What might happen if he got loose in your house or room? Use your imagination and tell your own monkey tale.

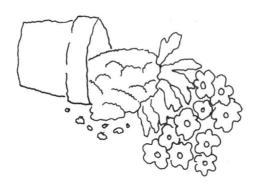

Little Monkey's mother said to stay out of trouble when he went out to play.

Little Monkey's mother said to stay out of
trouble when he went out to play. But Little
Monkey didn't listen! Now he is in big
trouble!_____

_____

_____

_____

_____

_____

_____

_____

_____

_____

_____

_____

Nobody Saw Me

It is typical for kids and adults alike to do something they know they shouldn't when they think no one is watching them. *Lazy Ozzie* by Michael Coleman is a good story to share on this subject. This animal tale can lead to a discussion of what we do when we think no one is looking. What happens when you find out that someone DID see you? How do you explain your actions? Write a story that tells what happened to you when you thought no one was looking.

I thought no one was looking when I . . .

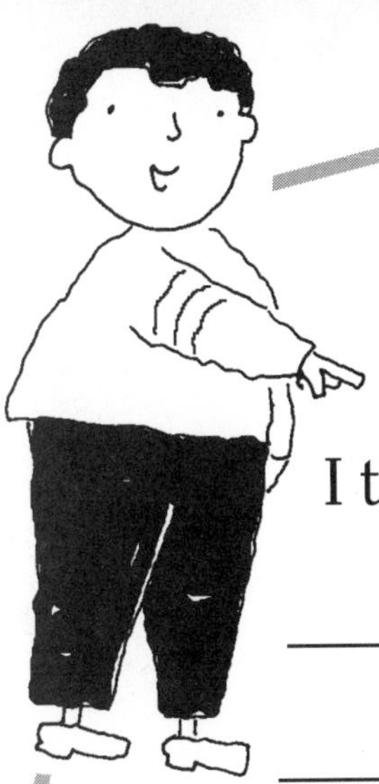

I thought no one was looking when I _____

_____

_____

_____

_____

_____

_____

_____

_____

_____

_____

_____

_____

Followed Home

The Boy Who Was Followed Home by Margaret Mahy is a fun story about a boy with a serious yet humorous problem. Share this story with students and then ask them to write their own stories about an unusual animal that follows them home. What happens? How do they get rid of the animal? What does Mom or Dad have to say about it? What does the animal do to their house or yard? Is the animal a big problem for the neighborhood? How can they remedy the situation?

I'm in trouble! I was followed home from school by a . . .

I'm in trouble! I was followed home from school by a _____

_____

_____

_____

_____

_____

_____

_____

_____

_____

_____

_____

My Collection

Most students enjoy telling about their collections. It might be a collection of race cars or Barbie® dolls. It might be rocks or shells. Some might have a baseball card collection.

Whatever the collection, students will describe it by telling such things as how many items are in the collection, where the items were found or purchased, which one is a favorite, and how long they have been collecting the items.

Everybody Needs a Rock by Byrd Baylor is an excellent book to share about the collecting of rocks. The author helps us to understand that the items we collect are special to us.

Let me tell you about my collection of . . .

Let me tell you about my collection of _____

_____

_____

_____

_____

_____

_____

_____

_____

_____

_____

_____

My Favorite Hiding Place

I n the story *Grandpa's Slippers* by Joy Watson, Grandma has places to hide Grandpa's old, worn-out slippers so that he will not be able to wear them anymore. She hides them in a closet, in a compost heap, and in numerous other places, but Grandpa always finds them.

If students have a present they have made for someone, where would they hide it in their house? Are there nooks and crannies that no one else knows about? How big are these hiding places and where are they? How did the students find their hiding places? What would happen if they told their sisters or brothers about their hiding places? How many treasures are hiding there?

My favorite hiding place is . . .

From *Daily Guided Writing*. Text © Carol Simpson and illustrations © Good Year Books.

My favorite hiding place is _____

_____

_____

_____

_____

_____

_____

_____

_____

_____

_____

_____

_____

_____

I Was Very Brave

Hattie the Hen had to be brave when she told the other animals about the fox in *Hattie and the Fox* by Mem Fox. In Leo Lionni's book *Swimmy,* the little fish had to be brave when he went out into the sea world without his brothers and sisters. The little girl who went into the woods to pick flowers had to be brave in *The Gunnywolf* by A. Delaney.

Each child has probably had occasion to show how brave they can be. Perhaps it was when they visited the doctor or dentist and had to have a shot or a tooth fixed. Perhaps they were lost at the shopping mall and had to be brave until a family member came to get them. Perhaps they had to stand up in front of their classroom and recite something in front of everyone.

Everyone has had to be brave at some time. Students will write about a time when they had to be brave.

I had to be brave

when . . .

From *Daily Guided Writing* Text © Carol Simpson and Illustrations © Good Year Books

I had to be brave when _____

_____

_____

_____

_____

_____

_____

_____

_____

_____

_____

_____

_____

How to Cook a Special Dish

This story prompt is designed to lead to the writing of a recipe for a special dish. Students will be expected to write their own recipes without the aid of a cookbook. To introduce recipe writing, examples must be modeled for the students to follow.

Share the book *Yuck Soup* by Joy Cowley. Ask the students to name the ingredients in the recipe. Use the overhead projector to model how to write the list of ingredients. Ask for the directions that would be followed to make the soup, and then model writing them.

Another good book that leads to the writing of a recipe is *Wombat Stew* by Marcia Vaughan. Modeling the writing of the recipe parts is very important so that students know what will be expected of them.

Books that lead to more traditional recipes are *Thunder Cake* by Patricia Polacco or any one of the many versions of *Stone Soup*.

After modeling several recipes, encourage students to write their own. They will probably know how to mix up a snack or quick meal from a time when they were hungry and had to find something to eat.

Recipe for . . .

Recipe for _____

Ingredients

_____

_____

_____

_____

_____

_____

Directions _____

_____

_____

_____

_____

_____

_____

_____

Excuses, Excuses!

Children make up excuses for a lot of different things. They will give you excuses for being late to school. They will have an excuse for not having their homework or losing a mitten. They will give you an excuse for the rip in the knee of their new pants. Whatever the problem, there's an excuse!

John Patrick Norman McHennesy—The Boy Who Was Always Late by John Burningham is a good book to introduce the idea of making excuses for one's behavior.

Imagine you have done something about which you don't want the teacher or your parents to find out the truth. What excuse will you give when you are asked about it? If it is a case of a missing homework paper, did the dog eat it? Did a bully take it away from you? What is your excuse for being late for school? Use your imagination and think up a problem you might have. What will your excuse be?

You have to believe me! This really happened.